From Sanskrit
to Brazil

Vignettes and Essays
upon Languages

By
Eric Partridge

Select Bibliographies Reprint Series

BOOKS FOR LIBRARIES PRESS
FREEPORT, NEW YORK

.

STANDARD BOOK NUMBER:
8369-5055-0

LIBRARY OF CONGRESS CATALOG CARD NUMBER:
77-94281

PRINTED IN THE UNITED STATES OF AMERICA

FOR
JOHN W. CLARK
of the University of Minnesota
IN MEMORY OF A DELIGHTFUL
COLLABORATION AND IN GRATITUDE
FOR MANY KINDNESSES

FOREWORD

THIS book constitutes a companion to *Words at War: Words at Peace* (1948) and *Here, There and Everywhere* (1950) in that it is a collection of essays upon language.

The shorter essays are attempts in a particularly difficult form – that of the verbal vignette. Of the twenty-five vignettes, four have not hitherto appeared; two others were published in a small specialist periodical.

Of the seven longer essays, four have not been published. Of these four, '*The Real McCoy* and *The Real Mackay*' and 'Westward to the Fortunate Isles', have, the former considerably, the latter drastically reduced, provided the material for my private Christmas Cards of 1951 and 1950.

E. P.

CONTENTS

I: VIGNETTES

A NOTE

During the period April 1949–February 1950, there appeared in *Leader Magazine* a certain number of very short articles upon word-history; the half-dozen others that had been 'set up' but did not appear, *Leader Magazine* being suspended in the Spring of 1950, are included in this section. The published form of these articles tended to be even shorter than the written. 'The exigencies of space . . .'

Here is a selection, including two rather longer than the majority, of those articles; nearly all in the original form, as they were before the sub-editors got at them. Scholars will, I trust, remember that they were written for a lively yet intelligent popular weekly: much erudite evidence has been omitted; some of the evidence that has, in fact, been stated, whether explicitly or implicitly, was selected in the interest rather of readability than of academic philology. Nevertheless, it is evidence – fact, not fabrication.

E. P.

THE VIGNETTES

FROM SANSKRIT TO BRAZIL

'THAT's a daft title! Reminds me of those Regular Army sergeant-majors who threatened that, until we learned to be good soldiers, they'd chase us from Aldershot to breakfast-time. Only, they usually said something much ruder than "*Aldershot*".' Yes; it *is* a bit daft, for whereas Brazil is in South America, Sanskrit is in time, being that ancient language of Hindus in India which supplies the acid test of whether any other language belongs to the Indo-European group, the most important of all linguistic groups.

Well, this is how it comes about. In Sanskrit there is a word-stem (or root: like *word* in 'wordiness') that means 'to shine': *bha*. From *bha* comes, through an old Germanic language, the French *braise*, 'live coals' – compare the Swedish *brasa*, 'fire'; from *braise*, the verb *braiser*; from the French *braiser*, two good English words, *braze*, 'to expose to fire; to solder,' and the *braise* of cookery, as in *braised steak*, or don't you remember?

The tree *brasil* or *brazil* is so named from its wood, which has a colour resembling that of live coals. From the tree we get *Brazil*, that legendary island of the North Atlantic which was fabled to abound in brazilwood. When the Portuguese navigators discovered the north-eastern part of South America, a region that did, in fact, abound in brazilwood, they naturally named it *Brazil*. Now, Brazil abounds also in *Bertholietia excelsa* (after Berthollet, a famous French scientist), known to you and me as the Brazil-nut tree. The mineral *brazilite* was found in Brazil; but the chemical *brazilein* and *brazilin* take their name from their source, brazilwood.

So, you see: from Sanskrit to Brazil.

THE WAY OF A CONQUEROR

IN 323 B.C., aged only thirty-two, Alexander the Third of Macedon, who came to be known as Alexander the Great, died at Babylon, partly of a fever and partly of a wound. He had conquered most of the known world and had been a considerable statesman, an enlightened man, and a tremendous personality. (See those two fine books, T. R. Glover's *The Ancient World*, 1935, and W. W. Tarn's *Alexander the Great: The Biography*, 1948.)

Of all great conquerors, Alexander has left the most instructive influence upon language, not only in the numerous cities named – some by and others after him – *Alexandria* or *Alexandretta*; not only in the popularity of his personal name (*Alexandros*, 'helper, or defender, of men' – originally an epithet applied to a Greek goddess), a popularity assisted by the fact that to the Middle Ages he was an heroic figure, admired throughout Europe, Asia and North Africa, a personal name with such variations as Turkish *Iskander*, Scottish *Alastair*, *Alec*, and *Sandy* – and, of course, the feminine counterpart, *Alexandra*.

Moreover, the Greek *Alexandros*, French *Alexandre*, English *Alexander*, has yielded at least two other notable terms. In the United States, *alexanders* (loosely, *alexander*) has, for some three centuries, designated the meadow parsley; we hear of 'golden alexanders' and 'purple alexanders'. The etymologists cautiously attempt no etymology. Yet, associated with the Near East (one variety being named *Smyrnium*, Smyrnian) and, by its colours, with royalty (golden crown and purple robes), the *alexanders* is rather obviously, I should have thought, *Alexander's* (*flower*). The other word is *alexandrine* as a term in poetry: a verse line of six iambic feet. This majestic measure befits a majestic theme; and during the Middle Ages it was used at least once in a French poetic cycle dealing with the exploits of *Alexander* (adjective, *Alexandrine*).

The name has left a pleasant taste in the mouth of time.

QUINTUPLETS, PENTAGONS, FINGERS and FIVES

T H E English words for the simple numbers – *one, two, three* . . . up to *nine* – look simple; yet their word-histories are difficult; almost as difficult as they are long. Recorded as far back as about 1500 B.C., they will perhaps be someday revealed as having existed at the time the animals were entering the Ark two by two, the elephant and the kangaroo.

To deal satisfactorily with the intricacies of the inter-acting histories of Greek *pentē*, Latin *quinque*, English *five* and the at-first-sight unrelated *finger* would require not a little essay but a biggish book. A comparison, however, of such early forms as Sanskrit *panca* (approxi-mately), Greek *pentē*, Latin *quinque* and, for 'fifth', *quintus*, Gothic and Old High German *fimf*, Old Welsh *pimp*, Old Norwegian *fim*, with modern *five, fifth*, German *fünf*, Breton *pemp*, Lithuanian *penki*, French *cinq* (from *quinque*) may serve to convince you that – whether they begin with *p, q, f*, all these forms being akin – somewhere further back than Sanskrit, they existed as one word in a common stock.

From that welter of words, let us take several of the more interesting. *Finger*, traceable only to Old English,

B

is probably related to Old High German *finfto*, Gothic *fimfta*, Old Saxon *fifto*, our *fifth:* each *finger* is one of a group of *pentē, quinque, fünf, five*: each *finger* is *one-fifth* of the main part of a hand. Compare the slang *fives*, as in 'He can handle his *fives*' or *dooks* (but that's another story – a Gypsy tale) or hands, i.e. he can box well. Perhaps the game of *fives*, whether the Eton or the Rugby variety, come from this idea of a hand consisting of five 'fingers'.

But what about *quintuplets* and *pentagons?* Whereas a *pentagon* is a five-sided geometrical figure, necessarily having five (*pentē*) angles (Greek *gonia*, an angle, as in *polygon*), a *quintuplet* is one of a set of *five* children born at one time (*quins*; compare *quads* for *quadruplets*): from *quintuple*, five-fold: *quintus*, fifth, and *plex*, as in *triplex*.

More difficult is that variety of the game of lotto which Americans have named *keno*. But watch: *keno*, earlier *kino*, derives from French *quine*, five winning numbers, the winner at keno being he who first gets five numbers covered in one horizontal row; the French word is simply the Latin *quini* (five each), itself from *quinque*.

BURNOUS, FEZ and TURBAN

ALL three words have an Oriental sound; all three words denote headgear, although a burnous is primarily a hooded cloak.

A European woman's turban is an emasculated form of the male headdress worn by Moslems in the Near and Middle East. The word was originally Persian *dulband*, a sash, hence a sash wound into a turban. From Persia it passed to Turkey, where, modified as *dulbend*, it colloquially became *tulbend*, which the French turned into *tulban*, then *turbant*, finally *turban*, soon adopted by the English. From the resemblance of the flower to the headdress, *turban* has given us *tulip*.

The Turks had a headdress of their own, the *fez*, a kind of domed skull-cap made gay with a tassel; not so very long ago, it was often inflicted upon British children. It takes its name from *Fez*, that ancient, both cultural and industrial, Moroccan city which manufactured it.

A *burnous*, often spelt and always pronounced *burnoose*, has a less obvious origin. Speaking of the far-reaching influence of Byzantium, the Grecized eastern capital of the Roman Empire, in the 6th Century, A.D., Henry St L. B. Moss, in his fascinating book, *The Birth of the Middle Ages*, says that 'The Berber chieftain was proud to wear the ceremonial *burnous*, the diadems, medals, brooches, and purple boots bestowed upon him in reward for his loyalty'. So the burnous is not originally Oriental, either sartorially or linguistically? Correct! *Burnous* is French for the Arabic *burnus*, but the Arab word merely reshapes either the Latin *byrrus* or *birrus* or the corresponding Greek *burros* or *birros*, credibly related to Latin *burrus*, Greek *purros*, 'fiery red' (from *pur*, fire—whence our *pyre*).

The Latin *birrus* has a diminutive *birrettum*, a cap: and *birrettum* has two notable modern derivatives, the Italian *biretta*, a square cap with three projections, worn by ecclesiastics, and the French *beret*, a round flat cap worn jauntily by all sorts of Frenchmen and tentatively by several sorts of Englishmen.

PEDLARS, PALMERS, TRAMPS
and HOBOES

THESE four classes of wanderers 'hit the road'. A *pedlar* or *peddler* is a *pedder*, an itinerant vendor carrying *peds* or baskets: thus the accepted etymology. I suspect that *peddler* is basically identical with *pedestrian*, one who is constantly using his feet (Latin *pedes*). A *palmer* was, medievally, one who, having visited the Holy Land, wore two *palm* leaves, in memory of the palm branches strewn by the multitude in the roadway as Christ triumphantly entered Jerusalem shortly before His crucifixion – an event commemorated by Palm Sunday. Soon *palmer* came to designate any itinerant votary. Some of these votaries, to lessen the expenses of the journey, peddled small goods: hence, *Pedlar* as the inevitable nickname of all men surnamed *Palmer*.

A *tramp* is one who *tramps* about the country; he disdains to work; to beg he certainly is not ashamed; *tramp*, of Teutonic stock, is ultimately akin to *tread*.

What then is a *hobo*? What a *bum*? A *bum* 'bums' or sponges his way through life; the noun comes from the verb, which comes from *bummer*, a loafer, which comes from German *Bummler*, an idler, a loafer; he travels no more than necessary. An experienced American hobo has thus differentiated *tramp*, *bum*, *hobo*: 'Bums loafs and sits. Tramps loafs and walks. But a hobo moves and works, and he's clean'; works seasonally, and is usually clean.

The word *hobo* is a mystery. The best-known dictionaries dismiss the word with 'origin unknown'. The four most popular etymologies are: (1) Latin '*homo bonus*', good man; (2) soldiers returning home from the Civil war answered inquiries with '*homeward bound*';

(3) strolling musicians playing the *hautboy* (later, the *oboe*) were the first hoboes; (4) and, as *A Dictionary of American English* and the present writer think far more likely (Nos. 1–3 are patently absurd), *ho, beau!*, later *ho, bo!* in address, where *beau* is an offshoot from *beau*, a dandy, and *beau*, a girl's male escort.

POLITICIANS: ELECTORS: POLLING BOOTHS

PERIODICALLY we hear all about those political panaceas served in yeasty bottles adorned with bright labels and filled with gassy waters: then, politicians badger and police control, but we, the electors at the polling-booths, decide.

Away from the promises and the insults, let us calmly consider, for a few quiet moments, some of the words connected with politicians, policies, police – with civic duties – and with hecklers at the hustings, the polling-clerks and their ballot boxes. Above all, let's keep the party clean.

Two main groups, politics in general and elections in particular, engage our attention. The former group rests upon two words: the Greek, and the Latin, for a city: *polis* and *civitas*. Greek *polis* originally meant a fortified place; then a town, a city; then a city-state; finally, a democracy. Modern democracy began in the Greek city-states. From *polis* came *politēs*, a citizen; from *politēs* came *politeia*, condition of a city-state, hence administration or government, hence Latin *politia*, Old French *policie*, our *policy*, but not the insurance policy, that being quite another story. When the Latin form, *politia*, passed into French, the sense 'government' remained until the 17th Century and then became specialized as 'maintenance of order within the state' and that soon became 'the public body, the men, enforcing it'. And whereas the Old French form *policie* reached England as *policie*, the soon arising alternate form *police* reached England as *police*, at first as a mere alternative of *policie*, the modern sense arising much later.

Also from Greek *politēs* came *politikos*, belonging to, or characteristic of the citizens or the state: whence *politic* and, by the English love of elaboration, *political*. The word *politics* has derived its meaning from *politikē epistēmē*, knowledge befitting a citizen, i.e. politics; the *s* has been added to *politic* for much the same reason as it has been added to *ethic* to make *ethics*. As *magic* yields *magician*, so *politic* yields *politician*, of which the earliest sense was 'schemer' or 'intriguer' – not unknown to-day.

The Latin *civitas*, an assemblage of citizens, then a city, passed through French, as *cité*, to England, where, after being *cite*, it finally assumed the form *city*. French *cité* yielded *citeain* (modern *citoyen*), which those inpendent-minded fellows, the English, transformed to *citezein*, probably under the influence of *denizen*. But Latin *civitas* itself derived from *civis*, a citizen: hence *civicus*, our *civic*. The basic meaning of *civis* is 'householder': it is the householder, not the rootless man with itching feet, nor the smart Alec flitting from flat to flat, who makes the good citizen.

The chief words connected with elections are *election* itself and *elector*; *hustings, platform, plank*; *heckle*; *ballot* and *vote*; *poll* and *polling booth*; *candidate*: these words, however, will be treated more summarily.

From Latin *electus*, chosen (*eligere*, to choose, select: *legere*, to pick, *e*, out of) has derived the verb *elect*; from *electio*, chosen part, our *election*; *elector*, a chooser, adopted without change. In form a plural, *hustings*, the *platform* (French *plate*, flat, and *forme*, our *form*) from which the candidates speak, has descended from Old English, where *husting* is a *hus* or house of the *thing* or assembly. The candidate's policy is also his *platform*, built of *planks* or the articles of his faith: and from the platform he answers the hecklers: *heckle*, to badger or harass with awkward questions and rude remarks, comes from *hatchel*, to draw flax or hemp through the teeth of a *hatchel*, a cleansing instrument. *Ballot*, originally a little ball used in secret voting, goes back to the Italian *ballotta*, from *balla*, a ball. *Vote* goes back even further – to Latin *votum*, a vow or a wish, hence a vote. *Poll* is the recording of votes, originally by counting the *polls* or heads of the persons voting; therefore a *polling-booth* is the place, strictly a booth, where votes are cast. The *candidate* is literally *candid* (Latin *candidus*, glittering white): a candidate for office in ancient Rome appeared *candidatus*, clad in a spotless white toga. At least, it was spotless when he began.

COIN OF THE REALM

ORIGINALLY a die for coining money, *coin* travelled to England, by way of France, from Latin *cuneus*, a corner, hence a wedge; some dies are, or were, shaped like a wedge. All coin is the property of the realm or domain of the *rex*, or king: Latin *regalis*, kingly, became an Old French noun, *reialme* or *reaume*: adopted by the English, the French word finally emerged as *realm*.

The royal nature of *realm* leads us to the *sovereign*, so named because it shows the king's head, the *sovereign's* effigy; literally, the *sovereign* is the head of the state; ultimately the word comes from *super*, above – compare the school slang *super*, superlative. Royalty has also accounted for *crown*, a coin bearing a crown as part of the device and yet another name that, adopted from French, has come from Latin: Middle English and Old French *corune*, from Latin *corona* (itself from Greek *korōnē*); the basic idea of the word is 'something curved' and it reappears in Latin *curvus*, curved. As, in happier days, a *sovereign* was companioned by a *half-sovereign*, so a *crown* is still companioned by a *half-crown*.

Florin also has been adopted from French; this time, however, not direct from Latin *flos*, *floris*, a flower, but from the intermediate Italian *fiorino*, little flower, the diminutive of *fiore*, flower: the *fiorino*, a Florentine coin, bore in its device a lily.

With *shilling* we break from the Latin-French-English triangle and transfer to the Teutonic: *scilling*, an old English word, occurs also in Old High German. Yet *scilling* has relations in Latin, Greek, Sanskrit, and the root idea is 'something cut, or hollowed, out'. Also Teutonic is *penny*,* with root idea '*pan*-shaped' according to one authority and 'something rounded' according to another; obviously the two ideas are but one idea. Of a penny, a *farthing* is precisely what its name says: the *fourth* part: Old English *feorthung*, from *feor*, *feower*, four.

Ending with a splash, we have *guinea*, another departed glory. It took its name because rumour declared it to be struck from gold brought from Guinea; certainly Guinea was, at the first coining (1663) of the guinea, noted for its gold.

---

* Compare O.H.G. *pfenning*, Old Frisian *panning* and O.E. *penning* or *pennig*. Note the *-ing* suffix.

PUNCTUATION and PUGILISTS

THE world's great boxers have not been embarrassingly famous for their punctuation, yet they owe their ability to the same source as that to which we lesser men owe the gentler art of punctuation. And what is more, *pugilist* and *punctuation* derive from the same root or radical or stem: a word meaning 'to sting'. I know that it sounds an unlikely story; yet it's true.

In Latin, 'to sting' is *pungere*; 'stinging' (compare 'a stinging blow') is *pungens* (compare *pungency* and *pungent*); 'stung' is *punctus*. Either from *punctus* or from the noun deriving from it (*punctum*, a mark made with a sharp-pointed instrument), comes the Latin *punctuare*, to mark with such dots as can be made with such an instrument, a verb that, by way of its past participle *punctuatus*, yields *punctuatio*, 'such a marking', with the possessive case *punctuationis*, showing how *punctuation* arose. You have only to look at a page of Braille to see the kind of dots I mean.

The Latin for a 'pugilist' is *pugil*, which is akin to *pugnus*, the Latin for a 'fist' and the origin of *pugnacious*: after all, a pugilist or boxer is one who, as his first characteristic, fights – or is supposed to fight – with his fists. A man only *fist*-tall belongs to the fabled race of *pygmies*; the word *pygmy* comes, via Latin, from the Greek *pugmaios*, often written *pygmaios*, itself from *pugmē* or *pygmē*, 'a fist', to which the Latin *pugnus* is clearly related.

The decisive factor common to *punctuation, pugilist, pygmy*, appears in the fact that, in *pugilism* or boxing, the *pugmē* or *pugnus* or *fist* is clenched, so that the knuckles form a ridge, a *pointed* weapon, with which the two opponents act *pugnaciously*, each dealing the other a number of *stinging* blows.

'VANTAGE ALL!'

The Language of Lawn Tennis

SHAKESPEARE, who mentions nearly everything, mentions tennis. That was tennis, properly so called; owing to the extraordinary popularity of its modern offshoot, the original game is now often called either court tennis or real tennis. As the turf is the sport of kings, so tennis used to be the game of kings (see Shakespeare). The origin of the name has been much disputed. Skeat, Weekley, and *The Oxford English Dictionary* mildly support the theory that the name (earliest as *tenetz*, very soon *teneys*, *tenys*, etc.) derives from *Tenez!* 'Take!' – the server's call. Webster alertly proposes *Tinnis*, the Arabic name for a medieval Egyptian town famous for its fabrics; the earliest balls being made of light cloth.

Played upon an enclosed court (Greek *khortos*, an enclosure), sometimes set in the open, tennis was in the 18th Century called also *field tennis*: whence the modified name and game of *lawn tennis*, originally – 1874 – but not for long *sphairistiké*, from Greek *sphaira*, a sphere or ball. At first, the real-tennis player hit the ball with the palm of his hand: hence the French name, *la paume* (Latin *palma*). Then with a 'bat' called a *racket* – not *racquet*, which is neither English nor French (*raquette*); *racket* is an Arabic word: *rāhāt*, palms of the hands.

With the successive stages, *point – game – set – match*, we are merely using special senses of words belonging to various activities, but *'vantage all* (40 all) and *love* are specific. *'Vantage* is short for *advantage* – compare *vantage point*; and *love* (a score of nought) comes from the phrase *to play for love*, i.e. for pleasure, not for a stake.

A *rally* is a 'keeping up; a concentration of energy in an interchange of strokes': to join (French *lier*) again (*re*) and again. It begins with the *service*, a ministering to the game, and may end with (say) a *lob*, a lazy-looking stroke with a name derived from *lob*, 'to let fall lazily or heavily,' the word obviously being echoic, or perhaps with a *volley*, which, unless it be a 'stop volley', sends the ball on a brisk flight: French *volée*, from *voler*, 'to fly', Latin *volare*.

'IT'S NOT CRICKET!'

FOREIGNERS and Americans profess to be amazed at the English passion for cricket; the well-informed among them never fail to remark upon the fact that, instead of saying 'It's not ethical, or honourable, or decent', the Englishman, not to mention the Scot and the Welshman, says 'Not cricket, what!' or 'By jove! that definitely isn't cricket'. *It's not* – or *it isn't* – *cricket* is the same thing as 'It's not playing the game'. *Playing the game* is synonymous with honesty or honourableness or general decency. I once heard a Frenchman, whose English was ten times better than my French, exclaim 'That certainly isn't playing cricket!'

The word *cricket* (the game, not the insect) is something of a mystery. The great *Oxford English Dictionary*, for which one needs a van when one moves house, states, 'Etymology uncertain'. The less massive *Webster's New International Dictionary*, however, seems to be quite certain that cricket, which arose during the reign of King Henry the Eighth (1509–47), himself too busy elsewhere to play it, takes its name from Old French *criquet*, a goal stake in the game of bowls, itself from Medieval Dutch *cricke*, a staff or a stick, ultimately the same word as *crutch*. In short, the old form of stumps gave their name to cricket as a whole.

From cricket, the English have drawn several of their metaphors. For instance, when a man is at a complete loss for either a meaning or a plan, he will, as likely as not, say that he's *stumped*: a batsman whose stumps have been hit is out. Very similar is *clean bowled* or *bowled out*, detected in a misdemeanour, hence defeated; the underworld of London was using *bowled out* (arrested) early in the 19th Century. Compare *caught out*, dismissed by catching, detected, caught, not *bowled out*. A batsman undefeated at the end of an innings is *not out*: hence such a book title as *46 Not Out*, the excellent autobiography of that excellent cricketer and writer upon cricket (and other games), R. C. Robertson Glasgow, whom, in the long ago, I watched in the Parks at Oxford, during the Jardine–Bettington era.

The curious would find much to delight and instruct them in the late W. J. Lewis's *The Language of Cricket*, a scholarly yet most readable book.

RUGBY and ASSOCIATION

BRITISH sport has enriched the vocabulary of the entire civilized and of much of the uncivilized world with a number of terms, such as *tennis, hockey, polo, cricket, Rugby* (football) and *Association football*. Someday, maybe, an aspirant to the doctorate will write an erudite and almost readable thesis: The Influence of British Sport upon World Civilization. Here is neither the place nor the space.

There are four – not three, as so many dictionaries tell us; much less two – kinds of *football*, a game called after the tortured instrument; *Rugby, Association, American, Australian*. At grave risk, I ignore the third and fourth, the one a mere offshoot from the first, the other an Antipodean mixture of the first and the second.

Obviously a football is a ball kicked with the foot. Without going into the details of their history, I may perhaps mention that the *Rugby* game began accidentally in 1823 at *Rugby School*, in the town of *Rugby* (not *burg* of the *rooks*, but *burg* of *Hroca*, a chieftain; *-burg* being displaced by *-by*), when William Webb Ellis picked up the ball and ran. And *Association* arose exactly forty years later, with the codification of the game by the London Football *Association*.

The slangy forms *rugger* and *soccer* are examples of the process known as 'the Oxford *-er*', a class of word-formations once extremely common among the undergraduates of that great university; thus: *Rugby* has stem *rug*; add *-er*, and, for correct pronunciation, a *g* – *rug* + *g* + *er* = *rugger*; and *Association* contains the stem *soc* (as in Latin *socius*, a companion, a partner); add *-er* and, for pronunciation, *c* – *soc* + *c* + *er* = *soccer*.

Three terms existing in both games may be mentioned: *goal* was, in the Middle Ages, *gōl*, which probably comes from Old English *gǣlan*, to impede or check (as, for instance, a movement); a *try*, from 'to *try*', was medievally *trien*, from Old French *trier*, to sift, to pick out – a clean movement from the mellay and muddle; and *penalty*, from French *pénalité*, from *pénal* (our *penal*), from Latin *poenalis*, adjective of *poena*, a fine or punishment.

ATHLETICS

S U C H athletic sports meetings as the Olympics and the Empire Games periodically arouse the public's never dormant interest in sprinting, running, jumping, vaulting, hurdling; in relay and marathon.

The centre of attraction is the *athlete*, via Latin *athleta* from the corresponding Greek word *athlētēs* (those Greeks always had a name for it): that word derived from *athlein*, to contend for an *athlon*, a prize – especially for a prize awarded for success in an athletic contest. Compare *pentathlon* and *decathlon*, contests in sets of respectively *penté*, or five, and *deka*, or ten, events.

The *arena* takes its name straight from Latin, where, literally 'sand', it also meant a sandy place for the fights between gladiators in ancient Rome; if not composed of sand, the place was covered with it to absorb the blood lost by the contenders; compare *blood and sand*, a phrase (Spanish *sangre y arena*) epitomizing the career of a bull-fighter.

Coming to the events, we notice that they consist of three kinds – running, jumping, throwing. The most picturesque throwing event is the *discus*, so called from the object thrown. The modern discus, weighing nearly $4\frac{1}{2}$ pounds, has descended, via the Latin *discus*, from the Greek *diskos*, the origin also of *disk*. Another Greek word that concerns us is *marathon*, that race of 26 miles, 385 yards, which commemorates the feat of a Greek athlete in 490 B.C.: he ran the slightly shorter distance from Marathon, scene of a signal victory by the Greeks over the Persians, to Athens, where news of the outcome of the battle was eagerly awaited.

Less strenuous running events range from long distances to sprints. To *run* – Old English *rinnan*, past tense

ran – is a general term, arising from the swift flow of a
river (the water *running* away); to *sprint*, or run a short
distance at top speed, is a specialized term, from Scandinavian. *Relay* is short for *relay race*, from relays of
horses in the old coaching days.

As *jumping* is of very obscure origin – it is difficult to
trace further back than Medieval Latin *jumpare*, which
I suspect of being echoic – we'll merely watch it; *vaulting* comes, via Italian, from the Latin *volvere*, to roll,
many high-jumpers appearing to *roll* through the air;
hurdling from the hurdles over which the hurdler has to
leap, *hurdles* being at first the movable woodwork frames
serving to enclose sheep or cattle; *hurdle* is a word of
the most impressive antiquity. Human hurdling is a
modern sport, devised in imitation of steeplechasing on
horseback: in athletics a *steeplechase* is a (usually 2-mile)
race over hurdles and other obstacles. True steeplechasing was so named because some conspicuous land-
mark, for instance a church *steeple*, was chosen as the
goal of the *chase*.

BEER, CIDER and METHEGLIN

BEER, the Briton's favourite and – formerly – most
nourishing food, made from malt (processed barley) and
rendered wholesomely bitter with hops, has several
varieties, especially *porter*, dark and strong and so named
because made for those porters – strong, not necessarily
dark men who like their liquor to be even heavier than
their loads; and ale, paler and less potent.

Both *beer* and *ale* belong to the Common Teutonic
(or Germanic) stock; *beer* may be akin to *bigg* or barley,
a word from Old Norse, one of the Scandinavian group

of the Teutonic branch of the Indo-European family of languages; *ale*, however, serves to indicate the often close link between the Teutonic branch and the Romance branch, for it is intimately related to Latin *alumen*, alum, the underlying idea of all the 'ale' words being that of bitterness.

The Teutonic peoples (and not a few others) are hearty beer-drinkers. Beer has a long history. So has *mead*, now the perquisite of a few enthusiastic conservers of a more jovial past. Its base is honey; either malt or yeast is added; a drink for he-men. Its name goes back to *madhu*, honey, in Sanskrit, a language flourishing in – very roughly – 1500–700 B.C. A Welsh variation of mead was metheglin: and *metheglin* is a Welsh word, literally 'physician's liquor': just what the doctor ordered.

Two other very English drinks are cider and perry; yet both came to Britain with the Normans, who brought many other good things. Although, unfortunately, hard to obtain now, the nostalgic *perry* comes from Old French *peré*, a delicious drink made from the *poire*, Late Latin *pera*, or pear. In Middle English, *cider* was *sidre*, adopted direct from Old French, which took it from Late Latin *sicera*; ultimately, the word is Hebrew *shekar*, strong drink, whence the obsolete slangy *shicker*, tipsy. Originally made from other fruits as well, cider among the French became specifically an apple product.

All this talk of beer and cider makes me thirsty. I must brew myself a cup of tea.

QUININE and CINCHONA

QUININE and *cinchona* form a pair that requires a very clear head; too many lexicographers and several etymo-

logists have lost theirs. Complete safety can be ensured
only if we start with *quin*, the radical or base of *quinine*,
the *-ine* being familiar to all of you as a medical suffix
or word-ending, as in *atropine*, *hyoscyamine*, and scores
of other words. We can, for instance, dismiss *tincture
of Queen Anne* (quinine) as being a figment of popular
imagination (folk-etymology, we etymologists call it)
and as dead as that lady herself.

Quinine, a remedy for fever, comes from the bark of
a South American tree. In the language of the Quechuans – Indians of Peru – that bark, like the tree, has for
many centuries been named *quinaquina*. The Spaniards
shortened *quinaquina*, either to *quinquina* or to *quina*;
more, they sometimes changed the Quechuan word to
quinoquino – and then, as often as not, shortened it to
quinquino – under the influence of that ubiquitous Spanish suffix: *-o*. Hold on to those facts and you are safe.

Now comes what has, to many, been a snag. In 1638
the Condesa Ana Chinchón, wife of the Conde (Count)
de Chinchón, viceroy of Peru in 1629–39, was cured of
an alarmingly recurrent fever by the use of quinaquina
bark. Grateful, she distributed the bark to many fellow-
sufferers. In 1642, the great Swedish botanist Linnaeus
complimentarily named the tree *Cinchona*, either in
error for *Chinchona* or as being easier to pronounce; anyway, *Cinchona* for the tree and *cinchona* for the bark, used
either as extract or as powder, have remained. Those,
too, are facts: but Linnaeus, perhaps subconsciously,
was almost certainly prompted by the Quechuan *quinaquina* or by the Spanish *quina* to think of *cinchona* at all.
At all events, *quinine* certainly does not come from the
name of the Condesa Ana *Chinchón*: quinaquina was
known to the Spaniards long before her advent.

The synonyms *Peruvian bark* and *Jesuits' bark* derive
from the facts that the Jesuit priests used it widely and

c

intelligently, at first in Peru and then throughout South America.

FIR, QUERCUS and CORK

THAT there should be any kinship between these three words seems absurd, but, like so many other things apparently absurd, it happens to be true. Let us look coolly at these three words – and at another, *Hercynian*, which may seem to have nothing in common with the other three.

But resistance may weaken at the mere sight of this much-modified quotation from *Webster's New International Dictionary*: '*fir;* Old English *furh*. From Danish *fyr*; akin to Old Norse *fyri*, Old High German *foraha*, pine-tree, and *fereh-eih*, the winter (or Italian) oak, Latin *quercus*, oak-tree, and Sanskrit *parkati*, fig-tree. Compare *cork*, *Hercynian*.'

You will notice that Webster implies that *fir*, *quercus*, *cork*, *Hercynian* all come, ultimately, from the one stem, a stem or root that must have existed even before Sanskrit, which flourished so long ago as 1500–700 B.C. You will also notice that four different trees have been named: fir, oak, winter oak, fig. Didn't the ancients know their own mind? They did.

The reason for the apparent confusion is this. All the early names, *parkati*, *quercus*, *foraha*, *fereh-eih*, *fyr*, were bestowed on that tree which happened to constitute the most important in the region concerned. The pre-Sanskrit root-word, whatever it was (many pretend to know, nobody factually knows), must have meant simply 'tree'; therefore, *quercus*, *foraha* and the others meant '*the* tree'.

But what of *cork*? It derives from Spanish *alcorque*, wherein *al* is probably the Arabic 'the' (compare the *al* of '*al*gebra' and '*al*chemy') and *corque* probably represents Latin *quercus*. The change in sense arose from a fancied resemblance between oak-bark and cork.

And *Hercynian*? In Latin, *Hercynia silva* designated a vast mountain range of ancient Germany; a range densely forested, notably with oaks: *quercina silva*, 'oak forest', passes, probably under Celtic influence, into *hercynia silva*, which becomes a Proper Name.

CORN and OTHER GRAIN

MUCH the same thing has happened with *grain, granule, pomegranate, garner, corn, kernel*, as we have, in the preceding article, seen happen with *quercus, cork, fir*. A Latin word – there *quercus*, here *granum* – has, or rather a remote ancestor of the Latin word has, taken shapes at first sight strange but, over the passage of centuries in time and of widely separated migration-routes in space, not so strange.

It is easier to work forward from Latin *granum* than back from *garnet* and *grain*. Apparently of Celtic origin, as so many agricultural terms are, *granum* (stem: *gran-*) means 'seed, small kernel, grain'; the basic form is ground down, ground small, as in Sanskrit *jirna*, worn out, in Lithuanian *zirnis*, peas, and in Greek *geras*, old age. In Old French, *granum* became *grain*; not solely from *grain* but also from Old French *graine* (the Latin plural *grana* taken as a singular) did 14th Century English obtain our word *grain*.

Latin *granum* had a diminutive *granulum*: hence our *granule, -ule*: hence *granular* and *granulate, granulated* (sugar). Three other derivatives concern us: *granosus*, grainy, has yielded *granose*, *-ose*; *granarium*, a storehouse for grain, has yielded *granary*, *-ary*; and *granatus*, provided with grains or seeds, has, through *mala granata*, grained fruit, yielded *pomegranate* (Latin *pomum granatum*, apple with seeds – i.e., a pomegranate), *granadilla*, the Spanish diminutive of *granada*, a pomegranate – and, through Old French *grenate*, the fruit known as *grenade*, whence, from its shape, the military missile, and – compare the obsolete *granate*, a garnet, and *granate* or *granet*, a pomegranate – a semi-precious stone, the *garnet*, Old French *grenat* becoming Middle English *grenat* or *gernet*.

The grain of a district is *corn*: that's why *corn* means maize in some countries, wheat in others, oats in yet others, rye or barley in others again. But how does Latin *granum* become English *corn*? Already in Old English the word was *corn* – with, by the way, diminutive *cyrnel*, which became Middle English *curnel* or *kirnel* or *kernel*; yes, *kernel*. Corresponding to *granum* are Old Irish *gran* (compare Welsh *grawn*) – Old High German *korn* – Gothic *kaurn*. As Middle English *brid* has become *bird*, so, in remote migrations, *granum* has become *garnum*, which has become *kaurn*, *korn*, *corn*: that sort of switch-over (metathesis, the learned call it) often takes place in language.

The adjective *corny* (originally American) in the senses '(unduly) sentimental; old-fashioned and stupidly obvious; stale', comes from *corny*, 'Of, by, for, in, corn' – hence, reminiscent of the country.

'BESIDE THE SEASIDE'

WHEN Mark Sheridan sang this song, you could almost smell the seaweed and the winkles. He did not, however, refer to the fact that it was King George III who rendered sea-bathing fashionable. This king took his bathes at *Brighton*, which in Domesday Book appears as *Brihtelmestune*, the *tun*, village or town, of *Beorhthelm*, a chieftain of long ago, with a name literally meaning 'bright helm'.

Less fashionable though perhaps more fun is *Margate*, 'Sea Gate' or *gate* leading to the sea or, in Latin, *mare* – compare *Weston* ('Western *Tun* or Village') *super Mare*, Weston on the Sea. *Margate* evokes *Ramsgate*, 'Hraefn's gate': the gate leads through the chalk cliffs to the sea. The sea recurs in *Bognor*, recorded in 680 as *Bucganora* and in 1275 as *Bugenor*, the *ora* or landing-place of some forgotten woman named *Bucge*. The resort became *Bognor Regis*, 'King's Bognor' (compare *King's Lynn* and *Bishop's Stortford*), in honour of H.M. King George V, who there recuperated after a dangerous illness. *Folkestone* commemorates the *stone* or rock of one *Folca*.

In *Bournemouth* and *Eastbourne*, the element common to both, *bourne*, means 'a stream' (Old English *burna*), the former being '(at) the mouth of the stream', the latter in opposition to *Westbourne* in Sussex.

Leaving the South, we may note *Skegness*, the *ness* or headland of *Skeggi*, old Norse and Danish name of a famous seaman or warrior; *Scarborough*, the *burg* or fort of *Skarthi*, a nickname, meaning 'Hare-Lipped'; *Filey*, place of 'the *five leahs* or clearings' (for homesteads); and, hardly least, *Blackpool*, simply *Pul* in the 13th Century, then *Blacke Pull* in the 17th, so named after a pool of a *blackish* (strictly, peaty) colour.

HILL, DALE and STREAM

WHEREAS the inveterately jolly and the incorrigibly busy-minded prefer the seaside resorts, the contemplative and the Nature-lover go to the hills and fells, the dales and river-valleys and lakes. But even of the latter, few understand the names of the places and districts they visit.

· Among the notable hills of England are the Chilterns, the Cotswolds, the Pennines. The *Pennine* Range recalls the Pennine Alps, separating Italy from Switzerland; the Alpine name derives either from Latin *penna*, a feather, with reference to the appearance of a stripped feather, or more probably from Celtic *pen*, high – present also in *Apennine*. The *Chiltern* Hills appear to be 'the Celtic hills'; the *-ern* part of the name preserves a Celtic ending *-erno*. The *Cotswolds* refer to the *wald*, Old English for 'forest, *wood*', of a forgotten notable, one *Cōd*, who gave his name also to *Cutsdean*, 'Cōd's valley'.

Dean, from Old English *denu*, stands independently in the Forest of *Dean*, 'the forest in the valley'. Two other notable forests are those of *Epping*, 'the *ings* or people on the *yppe* or upland,' and the *New* Forest (*Nova Foresta* in Domesday Book), created by William the Conqueror in his dislike of woodlands wilder than those of Normandy.

Forests have the beauty of Pan; streams, an irresistible charm for those who enjoy the sight of water threading the land about it. *Thames* apparently signifies 'dark river', as also does *Tamasa*, a tributary of the Ganges – a Sanskrit name surviving in Celtic; *Severn*, however, is a mystery, the Latin *Sabrina* probably deriving from Celtic; but *Avon*, another Celtic name, is merely 'river'

– *the* river of that part of the country, precisely as *Ouse* is '*the* water'.

Nor let us forget the North, with its dales (Old English *dael*, valley) and moors (O.E. *mōr*, morass, moor) and fells (Old Norse *fiall*, hill, mountain).

CONTINENTAL

To the five continents, some geographers add a sixth – *Antarctica*. The word *continent* has passed through French from Latin *continens*, that which contains, hence that which is contained, or rather from the oblique stem, *continent-*, which we see in the possessive case *continentis*.

The most important continent, politically and culturally, is Europe. *Europe* is the French and English form of Latin *Europa*, representing the Greek *Eurōpē*. Formerly it was fashionable to derive Europe from Semitic *Ereb*, the West, in opposition to Semitic *Asu*, the East: nowadays, the latter etymology is contested, *Asia* having an origin that, like those of so many very old geographical names, is 'a complete mystery', and the former etymology is, at least, badly dented, if not shattered. Perhaps, for topical reasons forgotten 2,500 years or more ago, the continent of Europe has taken its name from that of the Phoenician princess Europa, one of the many women led astray by Zeus; more probably, however, *Europe* is (I suggest) simply 'the Broad Land' – from Greek *eurus*, broad.

Africa is equally obscure. One ancient authority explained the Greek name *Aphrikē* as being '(Land) without Cold', from *a*, not, and *phrissein*, to shudder; another from Phoenician *afrigah*, a colony, much as *Cologne* stands for Latin *Colonia*, colony – *the* Roman colony in northern Europe. Modern etymologists, when they don't play safe with 'Origin unknown', derive it either from the name of a Berber tribe or from a general epithet applied to the Berber peoples collectively.

With *America* and *Australia* we are on safer ground. Australia is *terra australis*, the *austral*, or southern, land, from Latin *Auster*, the south wind; *-ia* is perhaps the commonest of all Latin place-name word-endings. *America* was named after the Italian explorer *Amerigo Vespucci* (1451–1512): the Latin form of his name was *Americus Vespucius*: treating *Americus* as if it were an adjective, we get *terra America*, land of Americus.

Antarctica is the Antarctic Continent, *terra antarctica*, standing *anti*, or opposite, the *Arctic*; *Arctic* comes from Latin *arcticus*, itself from Greek *arktikos*, 'of an *arktos* or bear' – in reference to the northern constellation called Arktos or Ursa or the Bear. The Arctic regions contain many bears.

'THE ANIMALS CAME IN, TWO BY TWO'

> The animals came in, two by two,
> The wallaby and the kangaroo.

THE *wallaby*, a smaller kangaroo, is by the Australian aborigines called *wolaba*; *kangaroo* is also an aboriginal name; and *wallaroo*, another kind of kangaroo, is aboriginal *wolaru*, mountain kangaroo.

The *puma* and the *panther*, the *cougar* and the *jaguar*. *Puma*, adopted from the South American language of the Quechuans, is merely a synonym for *cougar*, the great Buffon's mistake for a much longer name from the language of the Tupians, resident mostly in Brazil. Also of Tupian origin is *jaguar*, resembling – though heavier than – the cougar; the sense has been specialized from Tupian *jaguara*, any large 'cat'. *Panther*, especially in its popular form, *painter*, may loosely designate a puma or, less often, a jaguar; strictly it designates the American leopard, notably the black variety. Its name, however, comes from Latin *panthera*, itself from Greek *panthēr*, allied to Sanskrit (1500–700 B.C.) *pundarikah*, a tiger – probably, at first, 'the yellow, or yellowish (animal)'.

Animals even more impressive are the rhinoceros and the hippopotamus, both with names of Greek origin The *rhinoceros* has a horned nose; a *rhis* or nose, combining-form *rhino-*, of *keras* or horn. The *hippopotamus* is the *hippos* or horse of the *potamos* or river, *hippopotamus* being the Latin form of the word.

Then come those two odd creatures, the camel and the giraffe. Whereas *giraffe* has passed through French *girafe* and earlier Italian *giraffa* on its way from Arabic *zirafah* and was formerly named *camelopard* or leopard-like camel, *camel* has come from Latin *camelus*, representing Greek *kamēlos*, this last being an attempt at some Semitic word, perhaps the Phoenician *gamal*.

Likewise rather clumsy are the bison and the buffalo. Strictly, the *bison* is either the aurochs of Europe or the American version of the buffalo; in North America the name *bison*, ultimately of Balto-Slavic stock, was bestowed by the French settlers. *Buffalo*, however, has descended from Greek *bous*, an ox, through the name *boubalos*, an African stag but also a buffalo, hence Latin *bubalus* or *bufalus*, whence Italian *bufalo* or *buffalo*.

TIGER and HIPPOPOTAMUS

ALTHOUGH Mesopotamia was formerly a part of the vast habitat of the tiger, *tiger* does not, except in folk-etymology (pretty but inaccurate stories about the origins of words), take its name from *Tigris*, one of the two main rivers of Mesopotamia. Both beast and river derive their name from their speed – the lithe gait, the swift pounce of the tiger, the swiftness with which, for much of its length, the river flows. In Old Persian, *tighri* meant 'arrow', itself from *tighra*, meaning 'pointed, sharp', an arrow-tip being pointed. Whereas *tiger* has come to us via French *tigre*, *Tigris* comes straight from Latin and Greek.

Think of the Tigris, you immediately think also of the Euphrates. *Euphrates* is a very ancient name, used by the inhabitants of Sumer, the pre-Semitic kingdom situated in the lower part of the Euphrates valley, in the form *Buranunu*; later shapes of the word include the Hebraic *Perath*, the Armenian *Efrat*, the Persian and Arabic *Furat* or *Frat*. Compare the Greek, hence the Latin, *Euphrates*. In its oldest forms, the name appears to signify 'big river': the Euphrates is *the* river of the region through which it flows.

Watered by the Euphrates and the Tigris is the region known as Mesopotamia – 'that blessed word *Mesopotamia*', as a certain old lady would murmur, for the pleasure and the comfort she drew from the mere sound of that euphonious word. *Mesopotamia* literally means 'the land between the rivers' Tigris and Euphrates: Greek *mesos*, 'middle', and *potamos*, 'river'. Compare the Greek *hippopotamos*, Latin and English *hippopotamus*, 'horse of the river'.

FINE BIRDS

BEFORE I get properly started, I should like to forestall any 'nasty cracks' by saying that my own surname is topographical, not ornithological.

Ornithological comes from Greek *ornis*, a bird, and *bird* itself derives from Middle English *brid*, from Old English *bridd*, a young bird – a specialized sense long obsolete. The earlier history is obscure: but, despite the warning issued by *The Oxford English Dictionary*, it is not so very unreasonable to suppose some relationship to Old English *breden*, to nourish, keep warm, hence to produce offspring by hatching.

An over-all enclosure for birds is an *aviary*, from Latin *avis*, a bird. *Avis* appears sometimes in combination with a distinguishing name, as in *avis merula*, English *merle*, and *avis struthio*, which becomes Old French *ostruche*, which in turn becomes *ostrich*. Belonging to the same group as the ostrich is the next largest bird, the *emu*, probably from Portuguese *ema* (an ostrich); compare the *cassowary*, from Malayan *kasuari*, and the *rhea* or American ostrich, smaller than the African bird and less ornamental, but possessing the name of a very ancient Greek goddess, *Rhea*, mother of Zeus; and the American rhea or *nandu*, the latter name deriving either from the Portuguese name *nandu*, from Tupi, or from the Spanish *nandu*, from the related South American related language, Guarani.

Smaller, yet in some ways more impressive, than the ostrich is the *eagle*, Middle English *egle*, from Old French *egle* or *aigle*, itself from Latin *aquila* – compare *aquiline*, of a nose shaped like an eagle's beak; *aquila* seems to be akin to the Greek *aietos* (the eagle) – itself probably related to *avis* and therefore meaning '*the*

bird', as, in some ways, the eagle certainly is! Of the
eagle group, we may notice at least the *hawk*, Middle
English *hauk* or *havek*, Old English *hafoc* or *heafoc*, akin
to the verb 'to *heave*' and therefore meaning, literally,
the seizer; the *falcon*, used in falconry, was Middle
English *faucon*, adopted from Old French *faucon* or
faulcon, from Late Latin *falco*, (of a falcon) *falconis*,
taken from one or other of the old Germanic languages;
the *osprey*, a large hawk that swoops down upon its
prey, comes from Latin *ossifraga*, literally the bone-
breaker; compare the *vulture*, a carrion bird, which has
a Latin name, *vultur*, meaning the plucker, the render;
and the South American vulture or *condor*, a Spanish
word taken from Quechuan, the native language of the
Incas.

All of them in their widely differing ways, fine birds.

STORMY WEATHER

STORMS, tempests, gales; cyclones, typhoons, hurri-
canes: such violent disturbances of the weather are
picturesquely represented by the very words that denote them.

For instance, a storm sets up a mighty stir: and *storm*
is akin to *stir*, both in idea and in sound: they are
Germanic. The noun *stir* derives from the verb *stir*; both
stir and *storm* are related to the Old High German
stören, to scatter, to destroy – which is precisely what a
severe storm will do. *Tempest* has a milder origin, for
the Latin *tempestas* originally signified a length of time,
hence of weather – good or bad; the bad driving out
the good, *tempestas* came to signify bad weather, hence
very bad weather, hence stormy weather, hence a

storm or tempest. Clearly, *tempestas* derived from Latin *tempus*, time; even in Old French, *tempesté* meant 'time' before it meant 'tempest'.

A *gale*, or tempestuous wind, is admittedly of uncertain origin, but it appears to be related to Old Norse *gala*, to scream, and therefore to *yell*: in a gale, the wind screams and yells, sometimes with a strangely blood-chilling effect.

In 1848, by Henry Piddington in *The Sailor's Horn-Book for the Law of Storms*, a violent rotary storm was named a *cyclone*, either from the Greek *kuklōn*, moving in a circle, or from the Greek *kuklōma*, a serpent's coil. The weather-men's sense of *cyclone*, a system of winds, has given rise to *anti-cyclone*. A tropical cyclone, if it occurs in the China Sea, is called a *typhoon*, strictly from the Cantonese *tai-fung* or great wind, but early influenced by Greek *tuphōn*, whirlwind, typhoon – compare *Tuphōn*, father of the winds – akin to Greek *tuphōs*, vapour or smoke, and therefore, by the way, both to *typhoid* and to *fume*.

But the most interesting of all tempestuous terms is *hurricane*, which, altered from Spanish *huracan*, came from the language of the extinct Tainos in the West Indies; their *huracan* or *hurrican* bore the same meaning, it is true, but also the original meaning 'evil spirit': compare the *hyorcan*, devil, of the Galibis in Northern South America and *Hurakan*, the Guatemalan god of thunder and lightning, a god mentioned in Malcolm Lowry's *Below the Volcano* (1947), one of the three most remarkable novels published since the war. As *typhoon* to *Tuphōn*, so perhaps *hurricane* to *Hurakan*.

THE MONTHS and THE SEASONS

'I F Winter comes, can Spring be far behind?': as
Shelley pointedly and sensibly asked in his most famous
ode. Those who think of the year as opening with the
earth's joyous *spring* from the tomb of winter have both
reason and poetry to justify their attitude. The Romans
and many other ancient peoples began the calendar
year at or about the Spring equinox.

Spring, summer and *winter* belong to the common
stock of the Teutonic languages; Old English *sumer* or
sumor, ultimately akin to Sanskrit *sama*, season, is *'the
season'*, and *winter* (the same in Old English) apparently means 'the wet season' – compare Sanskrit *udnah*,
water. *Autumn*, however, has descended, through French,
from Latin *autumnus*, a word of obscure, perhaps Etruscan origin: and to say 'Etruscan' is equivalent to saying
'mysterious, undeciphered'. *Season* itself was originally
'sowing time' (Latin *satio, sationis*, a sowing); *month*, a
moon-season, is a time-measurement and is related to
the Sanskrit word for 'to measure'.

April, from Latin *aprilis*, was the second month of the
ancient Roman year; the old explanation, that *April*
is the budding, the *opening*, month (*aperire*, to open),
may yet prove to be correct. *May* is the month of (*deus*)
Maius, the great god, Jupiter. For some reason, *June*
was named after *Junius*, a Roman clan; *July* is easier,
for it commemorates *Julius* Caesar, born in that month,
and similarly *August* commemorates his hardly less
famous successor, *Augustus* Caesar.

Then come the *-ber* months: *September*, the seventh
month after March, from Latin *septem*, 7; *October*, the
eighth (*octo*, 8); *November*, the ninth (*novem*, 9); and
December, the 10th (*decem*, 10). The ending *-ber* indicates

an adjective expressing numerical order; with each of those Latin month-names, *mensis*, a month, was originally understood.

Of the three remaining months, we notice that, as *May* honoured Jupiter, so *January* honoured an ancient Roman god, *Janus*. *February* comes from the old Roman festival of purification, held on the 15th of the month: the *februa*, perhaps in relation to the *fumus* or smoke ascending from the burnt sacrifices. And *March* – compare *May* and *January* – honours the god of war, this being *mensis Martius*, month consecrated to Mars.

CHRISTMAS and ALL THAT

AN account of the many customs associated with Christmas would fill a book. This is merely a brief essay. Here, only one fact needs to be mentioned: in Britain, the vast apparatus of Christmas as we know it, although December 25 had for centuries been a joyous festival, has operated only since Queen Victoria came to the throne in 1837.

We are concerned merely with certain words characteristic of the Christmas season, the most important being *Christmas* itself. Celebrating with Mass the nativity of Christ, the early Church called the festival the *Mass of Christ: Christ's Mass: Christmas*. Strictly December 25 only, *Christmas* is often used loosely for *Christmastide*, Christmas time, the Christmas season. In Old and Middle English, *tide* meant either time in general or a season or a suitable time, an opportunity, this last sense being preserved (though few realize the fact) in the ancient proverb, 'Time and tide wait for no man'.

The word recurs in *Yuletide*, another term for *Christ-*

mastide. By itself, *Yule* means Christmas Day, but originally *Yule* merely signified a winter month, especially December. A *Yule log* (or *block*) is properly that huge log which was formerly and with much ceremony laid on the hearth on Christmas Eve to serve as a foundation for the fire merrily blazing throughout Christmas Day.

Christmas Eve, strictly the evening of December 24, often stands for the whole of that day; the day when parents furnish the *Christmas tree* with *Christmas presents* and the evening when children hopefully hang up their *Christmas stockings*. (By the way, the bestowal of presents at Christmas is peculiar to the Teutonic countries and to those others which are populated, in the main, by peoples of ultimately Teutonic stock; Latin countries and Scotland reserve this – or a similar – rite for New Year's Day.) On Christmas Eve, the *waits* are even more active than they have been during the week-or-so before. Literally, they are *watchmen*, those who are *awake* and alert and, at least nominally, musical. Their semi-religious songs are *Christmas carols*; and *carol*, descending through Old French from Greek, is akin to *chorus*. Carols, which should ring out joyously, sometimes sound like dirges: this tends to happen when the profit-motive, so alien to the spirit of Christmas, intrudes: a *noel* (this French word comes from Latin *natalis*, birthday: *Noel*, the birthday of Christ) can hardly be sung exultantly, thankfully, when the singers have their minds on pence.

Inside the houses, children at last fall asleep, only to dream of gifts to be brought down the chimney by *Father Christmas* or *Santa Claus*. *Santa Klaus*, the Continental form, is a corruption of the Dutch *Sant Nikolaas*, Saint Nicholas, who, a Bishop of Asia Minor, died in the year 345 or thereabouts, after having been famous for making gifts no less delightful than unexpected and who became the patron of merchants, sailors and, above all, children. From Holland the tradition spread to Germany and Austria, to Britain and to the Scandinavian countries.

Having slept off the effects of all that Christmas *cheer* or festive food, designed to add to the merriment expressed by smiles upon the *cheer* or face of every merrymaker (*chere* being adopted from Old French, which derived it from Late Latin *cara*, face – itself from the Greek *kara*, head, face), everybody takes, or pretends to take, exercise upon Boxing Day, when *Christmas boxes* or presents are given, by those who can't afford them to those who expect but don't need them. Now merely a Christmas present to postman, newsboy, tradesman's assistant, *Christmas box* was at first that small, occasionally wooden, receptacle in which apprentices deposited the coins solicited by them from their masters' customers.

So long as nuts and sweets, puddings and mince-meats, beers or wines or spirits remain, something of Christmas remains, until – on *Twelfth Night* (the evening of January 6, known as *Twelfth Day*, or Epiphany, a feast celebrating the conclusion, in medieval and early modern times, of the Christmastide festivities) – some parents gladly, most children wistfully, remove the holly and the paper chains, the mistletoe and the Christmas cards. But the wistfulness soon fades in the hope born of the new year. New Year's Eve has begun that salutary and – deny it though we may – welcome return to sanity and work.

D

ESSAYS AND STUDIES

VERBAL NARCOTICS

SOME years ago, the League of Nations instituted an inquiry into the drug-traffic; every few years, the Federal authorities of the United States of America vigorously carry out a drive against that traffic. But it has occurred to nobody to 'put the cops' on to the far worse, much more dangerous habit of resorting to certain words, either in order to obtain relief from the pain of thinking or in order to enjoy the unreflective bliss of being in the verbal fashion.

This habit is almost as old as speech itself. Speech being too wide a field for any writer to survey and for any reader to endure, we shall confine ourselves to a few of the drugs current in 1949 and procurable at almost any chemist's shop or drug store – for instance, our daily newspaper, the Government's reports and propaganda, the books and articles by certain fashionable authors. The four chief sources of these drugs against which no Narcotics Act has been passed are: Journalistic; Political and Governmental, including the Civil Service and the various Local Governments; the Armed Forces and the War of 1939–1945; Psychology, especially Psychiatry.

From a selection of the journalistic terms, I have excluded those which Mr Frank Whitaker has wittily called 'rubber-stamp words', such as *bid* (an attempt), *thrill*, and *dream* and *wonder* used as adjectives, all of them popularized – in part, at least – because, being brief, they go so neatly into headlines. From the far too numerous candidates, I choose *key* (almost a rubber-stamp word), *intriguing, glamour* and *glamorous, fantastic, operative* and, latest in this group, *rewarding*.

The first, *key*, dates from the War of 1914–1918, when men in *key positions* were reserved (i.e. preserved) and soon became known as *key men*, even more flagrantly with us in the War of 1939–1945. Nowadays, the most unimportant persons in the most unimportant businesses are pleased to describe themselves as key men. Nearly as old is *intrigue*, especially in 'That's most intriguing'. So long ago as 1919, a writer in *The* (American) *Bookman* was castigating this senseless synonym of 'interesting' or 'exciting' or 'puzzling'; in 1926, the late S. S. Van Dine mentioned its vogue, thus: 'Rather int'restin' or, as the magazine writers say, intriguing – beastly word'. Although the high-brows had discarded it by 1940, *intriguing* remains 'all the go' in suburbia.

Of the six journalistic terms, by far the most frequently used by women is *glamour* – or *glamorous*. These two words have become banal and trivial: they cover everything from true love to a sordid little affair (*nuits d'extase* and all that); from a beautiful scene to a pretty, especially if provocative, jumper; from moonlight on the sea to moonlight in Soho. Indeed, its misuse is 'quite fantastic, my dear'. By 1937, *fantastic* had firmly established itself, far from its literal meaning ('extravagantly fanciful'), in four very loose senses, 'impossible' and 'inconceivable', 'wildly exaggerated' and merely 'astounding', as in 'The German losses in Russia, even before they began to retreat, were fantastic'. By 1938, *the operative word* – see, for example, Nicholas Blake's *The Beast Must Die* – had become a phrase fashionable among the high-brows; by 1945, fashionable everywhere; and by 1948, Members of Parliament were talking of 'the operative clause' in this or that paradisal Bill. Poor *operative*! It has to do the work of 'most important, most significant; most notable; much sought-after; revelatory; helpful'. And now *rewarding*, which, fairly common in 1946, began its true vogue a year later, is shouting at us from every criticism of art or film, of drama or literature, and from every panacea-pamphlet that pours from the bull-dozing pens of doctrinaire utopians. 'How very rewarding!' means no more than 'How beneficial!' or even 'How delightful!' The word is still rather 'superior'.

To the general reader as to the scholar, the Political and Governmental terms form the least 'rewarding' and the least 'intriguing' group: *purge, executive, bottle-neck, productivity, hard* (and *soft*) *currency*, and *bracket*. From 'ridding a political party, or a nation, of members either treacherous or merely suspect', a sense implicit in the 'blood baths' so dear to Hitlerism, *purge* has been debased to cover any petty riddance. *Executive*, as applied to the manager of shop or factory or department, has come from America. A *bottle-neck*, or obstacle to *productivity*, was popularized by the Ministry of Supply; *productivity* we owe to the Labour Government; the Treasury has contributed to the growing vogue of *hard* and *soft currency*, sent to afflict us since the war. *Bracket* for a trade or professional group, hence for a social stratum or class, is probably the only gift made to us, since 1945, by the Commissioners of InlandRevenue: 'the lower-income brackets' and so forth: various groups bracketed together as having approximately the same income. But what is wrong with 'group' or 'class'?

From the numerous terms either fathered or fostered by the war, especially by the Armed Forces, I have excluded such too famous examples as *blitz* and *browned off*. In 1943, that dependable social historian and subtle yet always readable American novelist, John P. Marquand, remarked of the chief character in *So Little Time* that 'He was suddenly tired of all the new words –

"streamlined", "blitz", "three-point program", "blue-print" '. Whereas *stream-lined* comes from the manufacture of aeroplanes designed to minimize air-resistance, *blue-print* comes from the plans; by 1944 we were hearing of 'stream-lined girls' and 'blue-prints for victory'; by 1949 we have grown a little weary of 'blue-prints for a brave new world' that is brave but hardly new. For *blue-print* there is no excuse; for *stream-lined*, much, for it contains a happy metaphor – but what a pity that it's being so shamelessly overworked! The 'three-point program' (suggested by three-point landings of aircraft) did not 'catch on' in Britain.

During the war we heard much of *global strategy*, wherein Mr Churchill excelled. This globe is the world; hence *global* is 'world-wide'. Since, we have heard hardly less of *global trade*. From the Army, the Navy, the Air Force we have adopted *personnel*, as in 'The personnel of this firm amounted to six men and three women'. Why not 'staff'? A better adoption, though grossly overdone, is *target*, popularized by the documentary film, 'Target for To-Night' (1941). It seems, in certain circles, to have displaced 'aim', 'purpose', 'ambition' and especially 'proposed or hoped-for output'.

Perhaps the most interesting of the four groups is the Psychological. The oldest of the terms in this group is *reaction*, deriving partly from psychology and partly from chemistry. For twenty years or more, it has done duty for 'response' and 'answer', even for 'opinion' and 'sentiment': only a narcotic word could do all that. Nearly as old is *urge*, which covers almost as wide a field – 'strong desire' and 'eagerness', 'aspiration' and 'ambition'.

No less objectionable, no less brutally maltreated than *reaction* is *complex*, which now, among the unthinking, means no more than 'obsession', a very far cry from the correct sense, 'a person's entire range of ideas and feelings in respect of a particular subject', feelings and ideas not necessarily including the abnormal; *inferiority complex* for 'modesty either considerable or excessive' is a particularly insidious drug.

By the end of 1942, *integration* had ousted 'co-ordination'. In psychology it had been used especially in 'the integration of personality'. On June 29, 1942, in *The Daily Telegraph*, 'Peterborough' had a delightful paragraph, which contained the sober statement, 'Any M.P. who wants to keep abreast of the times is now careful to speak of "integration" '. More recent is *allergic*, which belonged primarily to the medical language of inoculation and has been transferred to psychology. The 1945 recension of *Webster's New International Dictionary* flatly classifies the sense 'antipathetic' or 'acutely irritated', as in 'He's allergic to heat', as slang.

Returning to the loans from psychiatry, we find 'Edmund Crispin', in *Buried for Pleasure*, 1948, remarking that '*trauma, complex, fixation*, and the like had long since been deprived by popular usage of all hierophantic mystery'. Although *trauma* (properly, a mental shock, especially one that causes a neurosis) is still hardly so common as 'Edmund Crispin' would have us think, yet *fixation* undoubtedly is common – among the educated, anyway – chiefly in *mother fixation*. Correctly used, the term has its merits; misused for 'concentration' or 'concentrated desire', or, a shade less reprehensibly, 'arrested desire', *fixation* is wholly narcotic.

Any term that prevents us from thinking, any term that we employ to spare us from searching for the right word, is a verbal narcotic. As though there weren't too many narcotics already. . . .

(Written in January and published in *Good Housekeeping* in June, 1949)

THE REAL McCOY and THE REAL MACKAY

IF you want to pick a fight in Chicago, just tell a member of either the sporting or the 'sporty' community that the American phrase, *the real McCoy*, originated, as *the real Mackay*, in Britain; if you prefer to be knocked out in Scotland, you have only to tell almost any Scot that the British phrase, *the real Mackay*, is merely an adaptation of *the real McCoy*.

As a repentant sinner, I should like to set forth the evidence available to both parties in this dispute. So far, the case has been rather one-sidedly stated, not only by Americans. I shall examine first the American claims and then the British.

Although *the real McCoy* did not win a place in the main body of the great 1934 recension – known as the second edition – of *Webster's New International Dictionary*, it will be found in the 'New Words' added to later impressions of that edition, thus: '*McCoy, the*. Also, *the real McCoy*. The genuine person or article, the real thing. *Slang, U.S.*' Apparently the original form is *the real McCoy*, and the other a convenient shortening. An earlier lexicographic recording occurs in Godfrey Irwin's *American Tramp and Underworld Slang*, 1931, thus: '*McCoy*. – Neat; good-looking; unusually excellent or genuine.'

In his *Phrase Origins*, 1936, Alfred H. Holt says that *the real McCoy* 'appears to be a ringing tribute to some honest and dependable Irishman of that name, but no candidate for the honor has, I believe, come forward'; there had, in fact, been two claimants proposed, both of them some five years earlier. 'Of course,' he continues,

44

'it may be ephemeral, but if it should persist, in the sense of something genuine and wholly admirable, people will be asking why we didn't locate Mr McCoy before it was too late.' Well, Mr McCoy is still very much with us. In *A Hog on Ice and other Curious Expressions*, 1950 in Britain but 1948 in America, Dr Charles Earle Funk has, like Godfrey Irwin before him, attributed the origin to the name of a boxer – whom, in a round or two, we shall meet.

American glossarists and others have variously discovered the origin of *the real McCoy* in the fame of a notorious bootlegger, in that of a cowboy and, especially, in that of a boxer. If the term arose early in the 1920's, it almost certainly owed its existence to the bootlegger; if about 1898–1901, then almost certainly to the boxer. Only if it had arisen later than 1925, would the cowboy have been a serious contender.

In *The Real McCoy*, written in 1930 and published in the following year, Frederick Van de Water has told the story of Bill McCoy, who, 'the founder of Rum Row off New York', was the liquor-running trade's 'most daring and successful exponent' – at least, during the period 1921–25; McCoy's illicit career ended in the latter year. What Van de Water has to say is important. Having veraciously remarked that 'the liquor McCoy's ships carried to Rum Row was always the best', the biographer continues, 'His erstwhile associates have epitomized his square crookedness in a phrase that has become part of the nation's slang: "The real McCoy" – signifying all that is best and most genuine. Eventually dictionaries may pick it up' – Godfrey Irwin's book appeared in April, 1931 – 'a verbal monument to one who played a hazardous game daringly and, after his lights, fairly and honestly. I knew the slang long before I met the man'; knew it, apparently, from 1922 or, at latest, 1923; author met subject some time after 1925. It is to be noted that, in the underworld of the 1920's, *the McCoy* denoted genuine distilled spirit (especially whisky) – neither adulterated nor diluted.

That theory, propounded in 1930, has much to be said for it; yet Godfrey Irwin, writing in the same year as Van de Water, had no doubt of the pugilistic origin of the phrase, and he too had been a newspaper man. But let us here interpose a few words about the least probable progenitor, the cowboy. In *The Glasgow Herald* of 27 July 1950, the Editorial Diarist has, under the provocative heading 'The Real Mackay', written: 'We have always felt a peculiarly Scottish resentment when in American films we have heard something referred to as "the real McCoy". Indeed, our admiration for that notable cowboy hero, Tim McCoy, has been shadowed by the feeling that somewhere near Reay he has ancestors who are turning under gravestones engraved "Mackay", restless at the distortion of their honourable patronymic' – a passage that has prompted the well-known columnist Ian Mackay to corroborate his brother Scot thus: 'The fact that the Real McCoy the American cowboy came from Reay suggests that his name is a corruption of Mackay'.

What then of the boxer? In his *American Tramp and Underworld Slang*, Godfrey Irwin attributes *the McCoy* to 'the pugilist, "Kid" McCoy, who was for some time at the head of his class'. 'Kid McCoy' was the boxing name of Norman Selby (1873–1941). He began as a welter-weight and in 1896 won the title from Tommy Ryan; outgrowing that weight, he became a middleweight – one of the best that ever lived; then he fought equally well as a 'cruiserweight' or light-heavyweight; and even as a heavyweight he proved to be formidable. 'Kid McCoy was not really a Heavyweight, although he succeeded in building himself up until he just exceeded the Cruiserweight limit,' says Robert Haldane in *Giants of the Ring* (1948) – to which I owe most of my information about McCoy.

McCoy, who was at his best ca. 1895–1901, owed part of his fame to his reputation of being 'a smart guy', an exceptionally good card-player, notoriously cunning in business, and unscrupulous; he knew what a gaol looked like from the inside. A shrewd judge of men but less shrewd about women – his matrimonial adventures were hardly less notorious than his cunning – he used his wits: and when he retired from the ring, he made good as a film actor. In short, a character.

An oblique tribute is this, paid by Robert Haldane: 'Perhaps the best thing [Tom] Sharkey ever did was to beat Kid McCoy, which, his weight advantage notwithstanding, was a remarkable feat'. Not in the least oblique, however, is this passage, from the same book: 'As a boxer he was unquestionably very good; as a Heavyweight, his greatest achievement was perhaps to batter Gus Ruhlin to defeat . . . in 1898; he also beat . . . Joe Choinski, Nick Burley and Peter Maher. One of his last fights as a Heavyweight was his defeat by Marvin Hart in 1903; but by then he was past his best'. In 1903, he also lost his light-heavyweight title to Jack Root. His decline as a heavyweight – not, it must be repeated, his true weight – began in 1900, when he lost in five rounds to Jim Corbett after 'a match full of science' (Haldane).

'McCoy,' as the same writer reminds us, 'has a particular claim to our attention, for he was the inventor of the Corkscrew Punch, in which the fist is twisted at the moment of impact. Like Fitzsimmons' Solar Plexus Punch, it requires a practised hand to use it, and, like so many "special inventions", it is rarely seen to-day. But it made McCoy a formidable fighter and a dangerous hitter.'

Between the boxer and the bootlegger lies the claim of being the originator of *the real McCoy*, for the cowboy is not a serious candidate. Frankly, I don't know to which the award should be made: yet, salutarily aware how long a word or a phrase may exist in the vernacular before it attains to the printed page, I should guess that *the real McCoy* arose ca. 1899 and therefore from the fame of that picturesque fellow, Kid McCoy. (But I shouldn't feel in the least surprised if that guess were to be proved wrong: we do not possess quite enough lexical evidence to justify an assertion.)

It must have become clear 'to even the meanest intelligence' – as it used to be the very rude fashion to say – that I assume *the real McCoy* to be, in itself, American. It is. But I suspect it to be an American adaptation, suggested by the fame and notoriety of either Kid McCoy or Bill McCoy or possibly both, of the British *the real Mackay*. The adaptation may have been unconscious or, otherwise regarded, an example of folk-etymology.

For some years, I took it for granted that the original phrase was *the real McCoy* and that *the real Mackay* was a British adaptation of the American – an opinion I recorded in the first edition (1937) of *A Dictionary of Slang and Unconventional English*. Then I found that *the real Mackay* had been current in Australia from well before 1903, when Joseph Furphy's novel, *Such Is Life*, appeared, that novel dealing with the last thirty years or so of the 19th Century – a fact I mention in the third edition (1949) of my dictionary. The Furphy quotation is perhaps worth recording here. 'There was an indescribable something . . . which made us feel that [sheep] station aristocracy to be mere bourgeoisie, and ourselves the real Mackay.'

What clinched the matter – the detail that defini-
tively proved the phrase to have existed much longer
than I had thought – was the fact (communicated to
me by the Rev. Robert Whyte, M.A., B.D., of Cape
Town) that, on December 14, 1886, Robert Louis
Stevenson ended a letter thus, 'My dear Colvin, ever
yours, The Real Mackay'; and on August 11, 1894, in
a letter to James Payn, whom he and Henley had,
many years before, confused with John Payne, he
referred to Payn as 'the real Mackay'. That Stevenson
could, in 1886, use *the real Mackay* as a phrase so
familiar that the allusion had no longer to be explained
– this points to an existence long antedating the year
1886. The Rev. Robert Whyte, born 1873, in Scotland,
recalls it as a childhood memory, a schoolboy memory
(George Watson's College), an undergraduate memory
(University of Edinburgh); the Editorial Diarist of *The
Glasgow Herald* states that the phrase amounts, in his
family, to a tradition; Ian Mackay thinks that, in
Scotland, 'it has been in use for over 100 years'.

In Scotland, the phrase has long – perhaps always –
been associated with whisky. (By the way, convention
speaks of *Scotch whisky* and *Irish whiskey*.) The precise
reason for that association remains obscure, for the
association existed long before any Scotch whisky re-
ceived the brand-name *the real Mackay*; but it may be
noted that, north of Inverness, lies the Mackay country,
which is also whisky country. Several Scotch whiskies
did receive that name; for instance, the firm of Mackay
& Company (established, 1903, in Guernsey) gave it to
a whisky in 1908 or 1909, and at least two other firms
have bestowed it upon brands of theirs. But the application of *the real Mackay* as the name of a brand of
Scotch whisky, whether as the registered trade mark or
informally, was caused by the widespread use of the

phrase to mean 'the real thing, the genuine article'; the phrase did not originate in the brand. The popularity of the various *The Real Mackay* brands, however, has probably helped to perpetuate the phrase *the real Mackay*.

After that necessary digression, let us see whether we can establish – at least, as a probability, for in these matters certainty can rarely be achieved – the origin of the phrase itself. Whereas in the United States the contenders are a boxer, a bootlegger and a cowboy, in Scotland they are a bandit, an actor, and the chief of the Clan Mackay.

The least convincing of the three Scottish claimants is a certain bandit who, named Mackay (or MacKay), was on the run. He sheltered with the clan, whose members, individually asked their names, replied 'Mackay', only to be told that they were not the Mackay wanted by the pursuers – not, in fact, the real Mackay. That is a Scottish folk-tale and not, I think, 'the real Mackay'.

The actor's claim arose thus. There is, in many parts of Scotland, a tradition that during the 1860's and 1870's the part of the bandit hero, Rob Roy McGregor, in the play or pantomime *Rob Roy*, exceedingly popular in Scotland, was played by a famous, well-liked actor named Mackay. My informant, Mr Alan Mackay of the Guernsey firm of wine merchants, goes on to relate that 'one night he was ill and to the intense indignation of the audience his part was played by an understudy. The audience rose and, amongst other things, shouted at him, "Ye're no the real Mackay" '; Mr Mackay adds, 'It was from this incident the expression came in time to be associated in Scotland with all that is good, genuine and authentic'.

The actor's claim is certainly superior to the bandit's

– every intelligent person will, of course, have perceived the possibility that a fusion of folk-tale and anecdote may have taken place – and it is perhaps the one that merits the adjudication *the real Mackay*. I, for one, should not dream of flatly denying its validity; that claim may be correct. But I do ask whether the theatrical incident occurred early enough to have originated the phrase. Historically considered, the chief of the Clan Mackay has, I believe, the soundest claim – a claim set forth, thus concisely and undogmatically, by Mr Ian Mackay ('the real Ian Mackay') in modest, good-natured answer to my not impertinent inquiry.

'I am afraid I don't know much about the famous phrase. . . .

'There is a tradition, however, among the Mackays that the phrase arose from the fact that there are two branches of the clan, the Black Mackays and the Red Mackays, and they were always disputing priority.

'It may be significant also that for many years the chief of the clan Mackay, who is Lord Reay, has lived in Holland and is a very prominent leader of the Dutch nobility. In Holland he is known as the Baron Ophemert. . . . Just before the war he came back to this country and has, I believe, resumed the chieftainship of the clan. He is in fact the Real Mackay, and it is possible that the dispute as to who was the Real Mackay, arose long long ago when his ancestors left Caithness.'

They left Caithness in 1627; or rather, Donald Mackay of Far did so. During a brief visit to Britain in 1628, Donald Mackay was elevated to the peerage with 'the title Lord Reay, to him and his heirs male for ever, bearing name and arms of Mackay' (*Dictionary of National Biography*). The family name of the 13th Baron Reay of Reay – in Holland, the Baron Mackay van Ophemert – is Aeneas Alexander Mackay; born in

E

1905 in Holland, he is indeed Chief of the Clan Mackay, a title he resumed before 1938, as we see by *Scottish Biographies*, 1938.

The case for the chief of the clan, with its turbulent early history (see, for example, Robert Mackay's *History of the House and Clan of Mackay*, 1829), is reasonably cogent, without being infallible. If that be the origin, the phrase may go back to the 1620's or 1630's.

We can now draw a tentative pedigree. *The real Mackay* was originally Scottish and is still used more by the Scots than by even the English, who were using it at least as early as the 1880's; it went to Australia, apparently in the 1870's or 1880's, and it probably travelled to North America at the same period. At first it was applied to men; by 1880 at latest, also to things, originally and, in Scotland, still predominantly to Scotch whisky. Such a firm as that of Messrs A. & M. Mackay of Glasgow – a firm that was founded in 1865 – exported its whisky to the United States, its liquor being uncontestably real Mackay; and the numerous Scottish settlers in the U.S.A. and Canada kept both the whisky and the phrase very much alive. But whereas in (say) Australia that phrase retained its original form, *the real Mackay*, in the United States it was transformed to *the real McCoy*, first under the impact of the hero-worship that, in the late 1890's, accrued to boxer Kid McCoy and then under that which, in the early 1920's, accrued, at least in New York State, to bootlegger Bill McCoy. Ignorant of *the real Mackay*, certain Britons – but no Scots – have, since about 1930, adopted *the real McCoy*. Recently, however, I have noticed that *the real Mackay* is, in England, gaining ground at the expense of *the real McCoy*; throughout Britain and the Commonwealth of Nations, *the real Mackay* is, in short, the predominant form.

As Americans have an iconoclastic yet unassailable right to *McCoy*, so Britons have a traditional, equally unassailable and almost immemorial right to *Mackay*. To Americans *McCoy*, to Britons *Mackay*, is *the real* form: usage has made them so.

(Written in August, 1950. A considerably shorter version served as my Christmas card for 1951.)

Postscript. Since I wrote this article, Dr M. M. Mathews's scholarly and exciting *Dictionary of Americanisms* has appeared. 'He consulted scholars and experts, from H. L. (*The American Language*) Mencken down to a lifer in a federal prison who told him about *the real McCoy*, from the real Macao – the uncut heroin smuggled in from the Portuguese island colony of Macao': *Time*, 2 April 1951. If one had no other evidence, this plausible theory would be seductive; and, as a guess, it is worth recording. Dr Mathews, however, gives this origin a less whole-hearted support than the writer in *Time* might lead one to suppose.

THE SPEECH-HABITS OF SNOBS

A Modest Note upon an Immodest Phenomenon

THE world contains far too many of those people who
have nothing to say – and who keep on saying it.
Nothing can be done about them: they're made that
way, as also are those who inevitably say the wrong
thing.

But there is another group, small in comparison to
the total population but, in the world's intellectual and
cultural life, important. They could be more important,
because, although most of them know what to say and
a few have something worth the saying, their manner
of saying it is unfortunate.

They speak like snobs; more, they speak as snobs;
indeed, they are snobs. That is rather a pity, since they
could be speaking as men and women, not merely as
ladies and gentlemen, and, above all, not as snobs.

This is not the place for a profound and erudite disquisition upon the psychology of snobbery. But lest the
ensuing remarks upon the language employed by snobs
should appear either baseless or rootless, it might be
well to mention that the least objectionable snobbery
proceeds from an exaggerated sense of privilege; occasionally snobbery arises from a sense of mere financial
superiority, and sometimes from a sense of intellectual
superiority. If snobbery arises from more than one,
especially if from all three, of those causes, it can be
a very unpleasant – or, if disguised, a dangerous – thing
to encounter.

Not all snobbery is social. Indeed, social snobbery is
by far the least dangerous, although it may often seem
the most unpleasant. Easily recognizable, it can, with-

out much difficulty, be handled – either circumvented
or nullified, whether by ridicule or by silent disregard.
Nor, of course, is all snobbery verbal. For obvious
reasons, however, only the verbal can be dealt with in
such an article as this.

In what ways does snobbery show in speech? It is
fairly easy to discern the speech-habits of snobs, but,
as in all such matters, it is anything but easy to pin
them down. The predominant characteristic of snobbery being the display of a feeling of superiority, a display sometimes conscious but usually unconscious, and
a feeling usually conscious yet seldom acknowledged,
snobbery frequently issues in arrogance, or in condescension, or in an arrogant condescension. But arrogance
and condescension appear far more clearly in bearing
and in tone than either in phrasing or in single words.

Snobbish speech can often be detected by the use of
understatement so frequent and so insultingly deliberate
that the recipient must be very thick-skinned or extremely imperceptive if he does not realize that the
speaker thus employs understatement precisely because
he feels that he is superior to the subject – or to his
audience. Most educated and most cultured persons
occasionally employ understatement; they, however,
employ it whimsically or apologetically, and they do so
from an innate modesty; they do it gently, not with the
suggestion of an ornately velvet glove over a haughty,
brutal fist.

Snobbery often issues in a playful euphemism – in
humorous or would-be humorous terms more offensive
than the simplicities for which they have been substi-
tuted. These euphemistic terms are more offensive
because they obviously have not been prompted by
modesty in the speaker, nor by consideration for the
hearer: intentionally or unintentionally, they express

the speaker's feeling of moral or intellectual or social superiority.

Or perhaps it issues in a marked triviality of speech. (Speech may, of course, become the printed word.) Like the rest of us, snobs may or may not have trivial minds. If snobs have trivial minds, their inevitable triviality of speech does not, of itself, indicate snobbery. No; I refer not to such trivial speech as springs from the quality of mind but to such as springs from a quality of character: to triviality employed, at first deliberately and then perhaps so habitually that it becomes 'second nature': to triviality that forms a weapon in the snob's fearsome armoury: to triviality that, by implication, is designed to enhance, in the mind of the hearer, the importance or, at the very least, the considerable merit of the speaker – a triviality that, quite explicitly, is designed to depreciate or even to snub the hearer himself. 'Oh, well, since you ask, I suppose I must tell you; but really, I cannot be bothered to give to this subject, which you can hardly be expected to understand, the attention it deserves, the nicety or the weightiness of expression it calls for.' That, or something like that, represents the clothing – the wording – of the thought, and the feeling, in the mind and heart of the snob.

To exemplify that tendency is almost impossible; the result would be even more trivial than the triviality it sought to render concrete. But most of us have suffered from the sort of snob who, to one who has met with grave misfortune, says, 'After all, they did leave you your shirt', the implication being that the speaker wouldn't care whether, in similar circumstances, they left him his shirt or not, and that the unfortunate fellow was making far too much of his misfortune; or from the sort who, to someone about to enter hospital for a notoriously risky operation, says, 'Keep your mind off

that handsome surgeon, darling!' with physical impli-
cations that can safely – and had better – be left to the
sophisticated imagination of the reader and with the
speaker's appalling self-revelation of an arrogant or
scornful belief in her superiority to anxiety and anguish.
That those examples are trivial and unsatisfactory, I am
aware. The reader must imagine the circumstances, the
tones of voice, the facial expressions; but then every
author has the right to expect in his readers an ability
to supply the full context of all dialogue.

Of a very different order to snob speech-habits is
'ancientry' or 'Old Englishry' or, as it may well be,
'Old Americanry' or, in its most aggressive form, 'Pil-
grim Fathery'. And I do mean habit, not accident; the
habitual, not the occasional, use of archaic words and
phrases; an intolerably knowledgeable affectation of
archaism. Americans can think of those fellow-country-
men who make rather a point of using terms evocative
of Old New York or of the Deep South of the planta-
tion era or of a Far West that has long since disappeared.
For me, it is safer and wiser to mention just a few of the
words employed by those English snobs who indulge
in this particular form of offensiveness. They *quaff* a
tankard of *ale*, even though it be plain beer drunk from
a glass; or it may be a *flagon* or a *stoup* of *sherris*, though
it be a Woolworth glass and grocer's sherry; or again,
they *slake* their *drouth* in *Oporto*, when they merely toss
off an inferior, headachy port, and then pretend to a
touch of gout, when it's merely rheumatism. They'll
go, snobbishly, to the pit of a theatre and speak of
mingling with the *groundlings* at the *playhouse*. To them,
every woman under seventy is a *wench*, and every child
a *poppet*. Yes, *egad*! – and likewise *faugh*!

Less easy to exemplify is that over-emphasized sophistication which the snob employs to convey to the hick

and the hoosier the impression of an immense and
esoteric experience of the most spectacular yet fashionable worldliness. Often this can hardly be distinguished
from a sedulously cultivated callousness or from an
ostentatiously 'hard boiled' or 'tough guy' speech. I've
heard girls using, through a muddled snobbishness,
words that, if they but knew their literal meaning, even
they, however moronic or however desperately 'smart',
would shrink from – or, at least, would avoid – using.
The very nature of such language precludes the putting
into practice of the adage 'Example is better than pre-
cept', although I may perhaps be permitted to refer
to that type of girl who, superior to the conventions
of ordinary decent speech because she thinks herself
superior to ordinary decent people, usurps the language
of men by using an originally underworld expression
and saying, 'I'd like to *lay* that guy'. You see what I
mean?

As towards sex, so towards liquor and gambling; as
towards life, so towards death; the sophisticate, whether
male or female, adopts callousness partly because it is
supposed to be smart but partly also because it implies
in the user an insolent contempt of 'the universal debt'
and an arrogant disregard of good, or even of common,
sense in respect of physical or financial health.

Less repellently, snobs tend to follow verbal fashions,
especially the *vogue* words and phrases of the wealthy
or the influential or the publicized intellectual or the
'fascinatingly' artistic. Whereas the *too, too* vogue of the
1920's and 1930's, as in 'That's too, too kind of you,
my dear' or 'Her hat was too, too frightful', is virtually
dead, the formation of compound adjectives in -*making*,
as for example in 'It was all too shame-making' or
'blush-making', is only moribund.

A more recent affectation current among snobs and,

it must be admitted, among certain others is that of the
employment, by the educated, the cultured, the well-
born, of terms of address formerly the prerogative of
what, long ago, one called 'the lower classes' or more
recently 'the working classes' (as though most professional men didn't work far longer hours than the
'workers'). Notably *ducks* and *chum* (or *mate*). But more
of these vogue words will appear in course of the following paragraphs.

Passing from snobs in the aggregate to snobs in social
and professional groups, we find that not only members
of Society ('the upper four hundred', or should it be
'the dominant 20,000'?) but also big-game hunters,
dramatists and dramatic critics, film actors and directors
and script writers, artists and art critics, writers and
literary critics, composers, executant musicians and
musical critics, doctors, but physicians rather than
surgeons, and psychiatrists rather than either, and,
finally, academic scholars: that all these classes and
professions and groups tend to become exclusive, hence
snobbish, in their language.

But before saying a few words about each of these
jargons, I should like to point out that the most dangerous snob jargon of all is that used by ordinarily
well-educated, fairly cultured, averagely intelligent
men and women. It is the most dangerous because, in
the main, it is unconscious. I refer to those people, most
of them well-meaning, who indulge in orgies of sonorous
or otherwise impressive words of the kind typified by
ideology, as in 'Whatever his current ideology may be';
by 'to *implement*' ('We trust that you will now see your
way to implement the promise you made last month',
where *fulfil* or, better, *keep* would be the unsnobbish
person's choice); by *protocol* instead of '(formal) agree-
ment' or 'code'; by *lebensraum* for 'room to expand' and

weltpolitik for 'foreign policy'; by *self-expression* (is there, ultimately, any other kind?) for 'living a selfish life'; by *integration* for 'co-ordination', as in the nauseatingly snobbish phrase, 'the integration of one's personality'. That last example trenches upon the snobbery of psychiatrists. Used by one psychiatrist to another or at a conference of medical men, the technicalities of psychiatry, its jargon, cannot be impugned: they are a convenience, the shorthand of speech: they share this characteristic with the special languages of all the learned professions and of all the skilled trades. Only when psychiatrists seek to dazzle laymen, especially away from the consulting room, by employing these highly specialized terms when they could, with a little thought, speak in everyday language, – only then do the psychiatrists become snobs. Still more so, those laymen who, by assimilating the mumbo-jumbo of their favourite psychiatrists or by assiduous but merely *ad hoc* study, acquire a knowledge – usually it's a shaky knowledge – of the simpler terms in the terminology of 'the experts'.

Among these snob words, wielded with a flourish or with a malicious self-assumption of superiority, are *the ego* (and, peak of knowingness, *the id*); *neurosis* and *psychosis*, often ludicrously identified; *repression* and *inhibition*, the latter usually misunderstood; *sublimation*, occasionally thrust at one by a person that, debilitated by excess, preens himself on having overcome his animal passions and likes it to be understood that he has left them behind him, whereas, in sobering fact, they've left him far behind; this *complex* or that, especially *the Oedipus complex* – oddly enough, the snobs have not yet seized upon *the Electra complex*; the various *fixations* and *compensations*; and, product of 'the Atomic Age', the *death-wish*. As a group of words, narrow in

range and, when strictly used, of rigidly specific application, this psychiatric congeries forms apparently the
most snobbish of all philological enclaves.

Only apparently. Perhaps still more rooted is the
snobbery of academic scholars: and by 'academic
scholars' I want you to understand those scholars who,
whether they are university (or college) teachers or
unattached to any learned institution, are either
pedants or else men and women so convinced of, and
so obsessed by, the excellence of their own scholarship
that they admit a meritorious scholarship in others not
at all or only with the most grudging and ungracious
reluctance. Not for them the attitude of 'we are citizens,
one with another', nor the realization (such as comes
to all scholars possessed of good sense and good heart)
that, so far as scholarship and probably the world are
concerned, 'the more, the merrier', certainly the more
the better.

The secluded and, far too often, seclusive septs of
scholarship, confronted with any non-University delver
into their field, in which they fancy themselves as
privileged proprietors, or indeed with any University
professor so audacious as to quit, say, French for
English, or even Greek for Latin, delight and lose no
time in referring to this impertinent interloper as 'a
gifted amateur'. Moreover, certain researchers into a
tiny corner or a little-studied, unimportant aspect of
history will, with the snobbery that tends to afflict those
people who have mislaid their sense of proportion,
stigmatize as 'superficial' any historian taking the
broad view or treating the general history of a considerable period. Academic snobs tend to speak of 'uncontrolled research' when they mean 'uncontrolled by us',
and of 'mere surmise' or 'wild guess' or 'unsupported
hypothesis' when they mean that someone has unfor-

givably exercised his imagination or his intelligence instead of circumscribing everything within the limits set by his erudition – or by theirs.

Artistic and musical snobbery, like that of the theatre and the cinema, depends sometimes upon the mysterious-seeming employment of terms that, divested of their specific value (their technical signification), are very ordinary and unevocative, and sometimes upon emotional terms so vague as to be almost valueless. For instance, *significant form* and *texture*, *the new theatre* and *atmosphere* and, originally, *décor*. But whether the term be precise or vague, it is so pronounced that, by the intonation or by the degree of emphasis, the speaker tries to convey, to the guileless he succeeds in conveying, an *esoteric significance* or a *Pickwickian sense* and thus to attract to himself an attention, a respect, he doesn't in the least deserve.

A few literary critics are nearly as bad. But they have a smaller snob vocabulary and are, in general, less objectionable. Truly snobbish is such a word as *authentic*, as in 'The emotion he describes is turbid yet authentic' – that is, genuine or real; and, if used unnecessarily, so are *stream of consciousness* and *interior monologue*.

Capital-lettered Society has its snob words, especially in the naming of rooms (*salon* for drawing-room) and clothes (*robe*, evening dress), types of home and styles of architecture, kinds of food, the *cuisine* itself, table appointments (*napery*, *carafe*, *epergne*), culture (*décor*, *le mot juste*) and entertainment. Then there are smartness (*chic*) and fashion (*le dernier cri*). Most of these terms are either unadulterated or mildly diluted French; oddly enough, French snobs 'adore' English words. But, not moving in Society I refrain from exposing my ignorance.

Yet of a sub-group, that of the big-game hunters and their talk of *on safari*, I have a rather more intimate knowledge. The genuine hunter, not the rich man of jaded appetite and boundless hope, is to be admired for his patience and courage, his skill and knowledge: and he may, whether out on safari or, as 'the hunter home from the hill' at 'The Travellers' or at a stag session in a Kenya rest-house or hotel, be forgiven for references to a *herd of giraffe*, a *troop of lion*, a *crash of rhinoceros*, or to *the brace of lion I bagged*, for he is then a Freemason speaking to Freemasons. But when, at a zoo, one hears a patronizing 'Just look at those two lion, Junior!' from a man unable to distinguish between a cougar and a jaguar, or between an eland and an elk, one rightly condemns him for a quite intolerable, entirely unnecessary snobbery; his son probably thinks him 'an unutterable ass' or 'a drip'. Much the same type of snob, he of the hunting field, always says that 'So-and-so *has a good seat*', not by any chance that 'He rides well'; revels in *masks* and *scuts* and *forms* and *slots*; and would sooner die than talk· of 'a pack of dogs'. (The right use of *hound* affords an infallible test of a man's eligibility.)

On a broader basis, that of attitudes of mind (and of an unfashionable and frequently denied adjunct, spirit), we may note a few odd yet extraordinarily revealing instances of verbal snobbery. Explicitly these instances are as shallow as implicitly they are profound; profound, not by intention but because of the unattractive depths from above which, all unthinkingly, the snobs raise a trap-door or a man-hole.

To pin-point no matter how few of these frothy superficialities and thus to focus a light upon them, to consider them at all and thus to invest them with weight, can be justified only because what lies beneath or behind them has its importance. *I couldn't care less*, and the slightly earlier phrases *I couldn't agree (with you) more* and *How right you are!*, began their careers in Society and until 1949 retained such snob value as had accrued to them from that source. The descriptions of World War II as *devastating* (or *too devastating*) and *shattering* (or *just too shattering, my sweet*) gained a certain spurious strength precisely because they were always rather snobbish. That attitude of mind which lent something of permanence to a famous wisecrack of the 1930's, 'In Boston we call it breeding. – How cute! In New York we simply call it fun', is snobbish.

All these forms of snobbery are still with us; they remain as sophisticated as ever, although usually somewhat less witty.

Many snobs are stupid; not quite morons, yet certainly stupid rather than intelligent. With a touch of acuteness not, among such persons, so rare as one might think, these particular snobs have come to make a virtue of their lack of true intelligence. Nowadays, it is regarded as 'cute' to be shrewd yet not noticeably intelligent. And it is very 'cute' indeed to be merely 'smart Alec' instead of genuinely smart. That, however, constitutes a form of snobbery unlikely to last more than a few years. After all, snobbery must have a comfortable basis of self-esteem.

(Written in November–December 1950.)

GENESIS OF A LEXICOGRAPHER

In his famous *Dictionary*, Dr Samuel Johnson defined a *lexicographer* in two ways. Literally as 'a writer of dictionaries'; not, you will notice, as 'a compiler . . .', for he was thinking of scholars, not of hacks. And idiosyncratically as 'a harmless drudge, that busies himself with tracing the original, and detailing the signification of words'.

One and three-quarter centuries later, Osbert Burdett, who met his death in 1936 by falling down an escalator but who had made his mark as a literary critic, and historian, of rare distinction and who was an authority upon mushrooms, published a volume of short stories, *The Very End*, in which he caustically yet not unsympathetically remarked, 'A maker of dictionaries is an active laborious creature, the navvy of scholarship, carrying his head backward and forward from one learned library to another'. Burdett himself was a very good scholar.

Well, every lexicographer would agree that, to be one at all, he must be 'active' and 'laborious' (that is, very hard-working), but few would admit that he need, unless he's a hack, be 'a drudge'; fewer still, that he is 'harmless', for the most damning thing you can say of anybody is that 'He's so well-meaning'.

Lexicographers differ among themselves as much in method as they do in style; as much mentally as they do morally; and as much in ultimate motive as they do in immediate aim. I cannot speak for other lexicographers; nor, even if I could, should I. They go their ways, I mine. Here, I shall confine myself to my own aims, motives, methods, experiences: and to do that I must, since this is not an academic disquisition, be frankly egotistic, although not, I hope, disgustingly egocentric.

Why did I become one of what some compassionate soul has called 'these poor, misguided creatures'? I could hurriedly answer: predilection. That answer is correct, it is also far too easy. A murderer might say the same thing. It would be more accurate to reply: training in (and by) life; training in literature.

If I believed in the Argument from Design, I should say that life has made me a lexicographer, or, more fully, that the very course, even the most unpredictable vicissitudes, of my life have 'conspired' to direct, rather than to force, me into this adventurous path and, perhaps even more decidedly, to keep me there.

Born in a remote rural community in New Zealand, I had, until I was ten or eleven, to find most of my own amusements. Luckily my father, a well-educated person, had a good, though small, library. He encouraged me to read. If I remember rightly, I needed very little encouragement. The first three books I read, and frequently re-read, were Thomas Hughes's *Tom Brown's Schooldays*, Defoe's *Robinson Crusoe* and Dean Farrar's *Eric, or Little by Little*, all set in circumstances and amid scenes quite alien from my own. The slightly archaic language of *Robinson Crusoe*, like the old-fashioned language of the other two books, sent me thus early (at the age, I suppose, of seven and eight) to a dictionary, with the result that, at even that immature age, I became accustomed to using these invaluable aids to knowledge and sources of sober, never-disillusionizing entertainment. Truth, although it may not be stranger, is both more durable and more satisfyingly exciting than fiction.

That dictionary and that reading stimulated an im-

aginative and, I fear, sensitive and perceptive child of
eight into the writing of three or four extremely short
stories. Then I never wrote another until I reached the
advanced age of twelve, when I began – at thirteen, I
completed – a novel of English Public School life, a
pleasurable task from which I was not in the least de-
terred by the fact that I knew precious little about
England and precisely nothing about Public Schools.
The odd thing is that I did not return to fiction until
1915, when, at the age of twenty-one, I amused myself,
by the light of a candle in a dug-out on Gallipoli, and
wrote a suitably gloomy short story of love unrequited;
nor again until 1928, when, with the pseudonym
'Corrie Denison', I published *Glimpses*, a volume of
short stories, which, to my amazement, *The New York
Times* reviewed favourably. To the novel, I did not
return until 1932, when I wrote and succeeded in getting published a pseudonymous, not at all good fantasy,
entitled *The Scene Is Changed*. To my very considerable
relief, both of these books have been out of print these
many years. Since then, the only fiction to which I
have committed myself has consisted, on the one hand,
of a short, intimate (probably much too intimate) love-
story, written in 1944–45, rejected by one shrewd publisher and since submitted to no publisher whether
shrewd or credulous, and, on the other hand, a short
story I self-indulgently yet not altogether uncritically
allowed myself to incorporate in a work that appeared
in 1949.

To the not improbably irate suggestion that this talk
of fiction may appear irrelevant and, in a lexicographer,
unseemly, I can only reply that I'm so unrepentant
that, the opportunity occurring, I shall, not improbably (and not entirely by way of parergon), write other
novels and other short stories; more, that I am so irre-

F

trievably lost to grace and decency that I believe the
mental and moral exercise provided by the writing of
fiction to be not only salutary to all authors whatsoever
but also beneficial to their art – yes, even to the art and
craft of a lexicographer. The ability to write about
words is a speciality, but so is the ability to write about
life; the man able to write about both is thereby en-
abled to write all the better about words in particular
and language in general and to bring to a dictionary
that breath of life which all too often is excluded from
dictionaries.

To return to the chronological order, especially important in any account of the genesis of a writer, my
family emigrated from New Zealand to Australia late
in 1907, when I was some four months short of fourteen.
The change from rural and, later, urban New Zealand
to urban and rural Australia proved to be something
of a shock, for not only are the countries sharply contrasted in climate and physical features, but also the
people of Australia are startlingly different from those
of New Zealand. The impact of those differences was
so great that, young though I was and therefore wholly
inadequate, I wrote in my otherwise deficient diary a
long series of notes upon the contrast in characteristics;
and among those contrasts I included those of language,
Australians having speech-habits almost as sharply alien
from those of New Zealanders as Americans have from
Britons in general and Englishmen in particular. But I
also realized and duly noted the fact that, despite all
those differences in pronunciation and enunciation,
in word and phrase and catch-phrase, New Zealand
English and Australian English had far more in common than in dissonance – as, indeed, have American
and British English.

From late 1907 until early 1915 and from early 1919

until mid-1921 I lived in Queensland. For the whole of the interval between 1915 and 1919, I was serving with the Australian Imperial Forces. I came, therefore, to absorb Australian English and, much more important, unforgettingly to acquire the knowledge, invaluable to a student of speech and literature, that even one language can and does change from clime to clime, from colony to colony, from city to country, from one generation to another, even from one social group to the next, and from childhood to youth to early manhood to middle-age to old-age: that language has its collective as well as its individual aspects, its deviations as well as its usage and usages: that it springs, not from books but from life, not from pundits but from the people: that it progresses or, at the worst, moves, not along narrowly, but only along broadly established lines of development: that it is almost as much subject to the vicissitudes of fate as are the lives of the most impressionable of men and women.

The war of 1914–1918; the war of 1939–1945: four years' service in the first, as a private in an infantry battalion – Gallipoli and the Western Front; and again four in the second, private and officer in the Army, aircraftman in the R.A.F., but, owing to age and indifferent health, all the time on the Home Front, although at first with duty quite exciting enough in London during 'the Blitz'. Those eight years out of my life were years very significantly in it: more, they probably were by far the most important, not only to me as a person but to me as a potential, then as a realized, writer – whether novelist or essayist, and whether philologist or etymologist or lexicographer. They brought me into the most human and intimate, the most searching and illuminating contact with men in both deed and word; that word, at its most deedful and urgent and fateful. In the

Combatant Services, I could and – in the main, subconsciously – did watch men's characters develop, and
their thinking, hence their speech, with them. Life
there acted as both a catalyst and a precipitate, which
is more than war can do of itself: most of us, resilient
and unthinking, rebound and recover from the mere
mechanical impact of war, partly because that impact,
however frightening, is so very obvious; from com-
munal life, lived in such circumstances, we never rebound, never 'recover', partly because we seldom think
about it, that life being, as it were, the air we breathe,
the ambience of our existences. Some, of course, pay a
price so heavy that the benefits do not accrue. But they
are not many. In its general aspects a curse and a dis-
aster, war should, for all such reflective individuals as
suffer no irremediable damage, turn out to be, in its
total effect, a blessing. It did for me; perhaps I was
lucky. Certainly I account myself fortunate to have met
with those experiences which did come my way. Certainly I've paid a price: but the price was comparatively
low.

Neither in 1914–1918 nor in 1939–1945 did I plan
to 'cash in on' a world-wide misfortune. But I did have
to 'get it out of my system'. This I succeeded in doing
by writing either about or near them. The earlier conflict produced, long after, *Three Personal Records*, 1929 in
England, 1930 in America – published, that is, during
the worst of the depression, yet long out of print; *Songs
and Slang of the British Soldier*, now hard to find; and
A Martial Medley, an anthology of original articles and
stories, now more than merely hard to find. All were
collaborative works. So is *A Dictionary of Forces' Slang:
1939–1945*, happily in print. Two of those books are
dictionaries; the other two, mainly autobiographical.

On returning from World War I, I completed my

long-interrupted course at the University of Queensland, and in 1921 I went, on a travelling fellowship, to the University of Oxford, where I took a B.Litt. with a comparative study in French and English literature. Some research had to be done in Paris, where, on and off, I spent much time until about 1934. At Oxford, I met, and enjoyed the counsel of, three outstanding men: Dr. A. J. Carlyle, the Puck of scholarship; Professor George Gordon, later President of Magdalen College; and Professor H. C. K. Wyld, author of several very well-known books upon English language. All of them are dead. To my two years at Oxford I owe an unrepayable debt.

During the two years beginning in September, 1925, I was a lecturer in English literature at the Universities of Manchester and London. At this point, therefore, I may fittingly interpolate a brief mention of the second of the two trainings that have contributed to the genesis of a lexicographer: life and literature. One cannot honestly pretend to a knowledge of any civilized language unless one has an adequate knowledge of the literature. Whatever my failings, I can at least say that I have continuously read works of literature ever since I unintentionally started off with *Robinson Crusoe*. My first two published books were *Eighteenth-Century English Romantic Poetry* and *The French Romantics' Knowledge of English Literature*, both issued in Paris in 1924. From then until 1932 inclusive, my publications consisted mainly of studies in English literature. Since 1931, however, I have worked mostly at one or other phase of English language, the exception being *A Journey to the Edge of Morning*, a volume of essays published (although not in America) in 1946. This almost life-long association with literature has helped to preserve me from the morass of ingrown philology; that is, from such philo-

logical writing or compilation as seems to imply a belief
that words and language itself have an existence apart
from the countless millions of men and women who
originated and developed the words and languages.

But to revert, once more, to chronology. In 1927 I
founded and until late in 1931 controlled a small pub-
lishing firm known as The Scholartis Press. In 1929 it
issued *Three Personal Records of the War*, by R. H. Mot-
tram, John Easton and myself. As a result of reading
that book, John Brophy suggested that he and I should
collaborate in *Songs and Slang*, which appeared in June,
1930. While we were working upon it, we both had
occasion to consult Captain Francis Grose's *A Classical
Dictionary of the Vulgar Tongue* (1785). Mr Brophy urged
me to publish an edition of 'Grose', with a biographical
essay and a copious commentary. I did. The book,
issued in 1931, has for several years been out of print
and is now obtainable only at a price I myself am
assuredly not prepared to pay. Those two works at-
tracted the attention of a far-seeing publisher, who in-
vited me to write a study of slang and, that completed,
a dictionary of slang.

Three Personal Records started a train that has run for
some years. But I had been profoundly interested in
language ever since 1907; the war brought above the
surface a seed that had germinated long before. To
Eighteenth-Century Romantic Poetry I added an appendix
dealing with the neologisms occurring in the verses of
the poets concerned. Philologically I owe most to the
works of Henry Bradley, Logan Pearsall Smith, H. C. K.
Wyld and Ernest Weekley; I owe much also to the
guidance of J. J. Stable, my old Professor of English at
the University of Queensland.

Of my development in lexicography, however, there
remains something to say – something to add to those

early indications. My first really big piece of work was *A Dictionary of Slang and Unconventional English*, published in February, 1937, second edition in 1938, and the third, very much enlarged, late in 1949.* The second is *A Dictionary of the Underworld, British and American*, commenced in October, 1936 and completed in 1949. And they *were* big, for both of them cover a period of more than four centuries. Other works have appeared since I 'turned author' in December, 1931, the most successful being, I suppose, *Usage and Abusage*, appearing (October, 1942) in America nearly four-and-a-half years before it did in England; *The World of Words*, an exercise in popularization; *A Dictionary of Clichés*, conceived in jest, borne mirthfully, and born in September, 1940, at the height of 'The London Blitz'; and *Name into Word*, which also was great fun to write. And there were three collections of philological essays – a form to which I am distressingly addicted. The first has long been out of print; the other two are *Words at War: Words at Peace*, 1948, and *Here, There and Everywhere*, first and second editions in 1950.

The most cursory consideration of the books mentioned above may serve to show that I like to deal as much with language in general as with particular aspects. That affection underlies the book on which I have recently been working and which will (we hope) appear† during the Festival of Britain: *A History of British and American English since 1900*, where I handle both the general and the British themes and John W. Clark, Associate Professor of English in the University of Minnesota, the American. But what fascinates me the most is etymology. Since mid-1948 I have, with the exception just mentioned, been engaged upon an enter-

---

* Since then, the fourth edition has appeared; it is virtually the same as the third.　　　　　† It did.

prise that will, I fear, keep me out of mischief until
1957 or perhaps 1958 or even 1959. An etymological
dictionary of English, British and American, upon
entirely new lines.

For this work, I shall require not only all the courage
and resources that can be afforded by a powerful predilection, by knowledge, and by industry, patience
and perseverance, but also an enduring, open-minded
enthusiasm – ingenuity – and imagination rather than
mere fancy. One cannot exemplify most of those re-
quisites, but one can perhaps indicate what is meant, in
lexicography, by ingenuity and imagination.

Established for some 150 years as the commonest of
the British slang terms for 'sixpence' is *tanner*, dismissed
by all the most authoritative dictionaries as of 'uncertain, or obscure, origin'. Origins in Latin and Romany
can be ignored. Perhaps I may be allowed to quote
from 'Neither Cricket nor Philology . . .', an essay included in a self-anthology, *A Covey of Partridge*, published
in 1937 but long out of print. 'The origin I submit is
more fantastic; but many slang words are of an origin
that at first seems fantastic. As early as the late seven-
teenth century, there was a slang word for sixpence
[– it survived until about 1820]: and that was *simon* or
Simon. I don't pretend to know the origin of *Simon*,
though it is probably a fanciful name, precisely as *bob*
(a shilling) may be *Bob* and *susie* (sixpence) may be
Susie; but *tanner* may well have been suggested by that
Biblical passage which later accounted for "the old
joke . . . about St Peter's banking transaction, when
he 'lodged with one Simon a tanner' " (*Household Words*,
June 20, 1885)'. The exact passages in *Acts*, *x*, 6 and 32,
are respectively: 'He [Peter] lodgeth with one Simon a
tanner' and 'He [Peter] lodgeth in the house of Simon
a tanner': in both of which, modern punctuation would

put a comma after 'Simon'; the more relevant passage is 'He lodgeth with one Simon a tanner'. But to continue with the quotation from *A Covey*: 'Incredible? Well, I won't argue about it further than to equate the semantics; thus:

> "one Simon a tanner"
> 1 Simon = a tanner
> a sixpence = a Tanner
> hence,   a Tanner = sixpence.'

Having been at first derided for excessive ingenuity, that proposed etymology has gained ground. So has the following, which exemplifies imagination – or so I like to think. The *tarot* pack of cards has caused much trouble. *The Oxford English Dictionary* adduces such European forms as Italian *tarocchi* and Old French *tarau* or *tarault*, Modern *tarot*, the form adopted by English, but states that the word is 'of unknown origin'; so do 'Webster' and 'Weekley'. To quote again from 'Neither Cricket nor Philology . . .' (where 'not cricket' alludes to the English statutory condemnation of anything dishonest): – 'These cards have, for centuries, been used in fortune-telling; originally and still mainly by the Gypsies. . . . Of the 78 cards of a Tarot pack, 52 are those of an ordinary pack; only 26 are essential Tarot. These 26 represent powers that are friendly, but also, and more, powers that are inimical to man. By a wholly unphilological reasoning I said to myself: "Fortune-telling cards; Gypsies; coming from India, but – witness their old name, *Egyptians* – almost certainly connected with Egypt at one time; so have a look at Wallis Budge". That great Egyptologist's *Egyptian Dictionary* . . . contains . . . *taru* . . . "fiends, demons, devils, enemies". (He also has "*Tar* . . . a fiend . . .", as well

as a host of other terms cognate with *Taru*.) There is
not, I think, much need to gild Egyptian gold', especially as Old French *tarau* corresponds so closely to *taru*,
which, let me repeat, is a plural.

'Yes! But how, in general, does a lexicographer go
about his work?' I cannot answer for others, although
I do most heartily disagree with the late Professor W. W.
Skeat's reputed, although probably apocryphal, dictum
that if he failed to solve an etymology in twenty minutes,
he left it alone or, in other words, discarded it – with
the label 'Origin obscure'.

Since generalizations can become very tedious, I shall
briefly tell how I went about two of my dictionaries.

For *A Dictionary of Slang and Unconventional English*, as
for *A Dictionary of the Underworld*, I spent three well-
occupied weeks in planning the book: the period to be
covered; the scope – involving the solution of some very
knotty problems of delimitation and classification; the
alphabetical system to be followed, there being, con-
trary to general belief, two systems, each with much
to recommend it – the absolute, as in 'Webster', and
the something-before-nothing, as in these two dictionaries of mine; the order of procedure within every single
entry – whether, for instance, etymology should come
first or last, and to what extent, if any, quotations
should be used; and many others, several of them too
erudite for mention here. For the earlier work, I decided
to deal with the slang, colloquialisms, catch-phrases,
and so forth, of the entire British Commonwealth of
Nations; for the latter, with the underworld speech of
the United States as well. For both, I read widely,
moved in many circles, and listened hard; necessarily,
I listened very discreetly, wherever I might be prose-
cuting my researches.

That precaution held doubly good for *Underworld*.

(For America, by the way, I had the assistance of some very able and suitable persons, both during and after my search in literally every American book and periodical available in Britain. All collation, all etymological work fell to me, although occasionally I had to apply to an American for the solution of an etymology.) Only a little of the underworld material that came to me direct was in written form, professional criminals being, with the exception of confidence tricksters ('con men'), notoriously inept with the pen, even 'penmen' or 'scratchers' being useless – outside of forgery. Luckily, famous criminals have employed 'ghosts', and they and other criminals have frequently been tapped by journalists and authors; prison chaplains and governors, or wardens, are, to coin a phrase, mines of information; police officers, especially detectives, pick up many words and phrases; tramps and hoboes, whether ex-professional or amateur, tend much more than criminals to write of their experiences; special investigators into prostitution and the drug-traffic – that is, those of them who take their work seriously and are engaged therein for long periods – learn much of the cant (the philologists' term for 'language of the underworld') used by the purveyors and their customers; police-court proceedings are occasionally helpful. That is an incomplete though not a grossly inadequate list of the more accessible sources available to a researcher into cant.

But he who deals, or professes to deal, directly with the underworld has to be very careful. Criminals are naturally suspicious of a stranger: and usually they either withhold information or supply 'phoney' material. But unconsciously they let things out, for the very simple reason that, unless (as is rare) they are well-educated and unless (as is equally rare) they are speech-conscious, they are often unaware that a term or a phrase does, in fact, belong to cant. When a criminal has been using an underworld expression for five or ten years, he forgets when and, above all, where he acquired it. More than one British, and more than one American, journalist and social worker and philologist have had their legs pulled. Rarely will a 'working' criminal impart the required information; when he does, it is because he trusts the inquirer not to divulge names or other police-useful details; that confidence has to be earned. Ex-criminals, however, are less reticent. As for the dating and the etymology of material supplied by criminals (and hoboes), whether active or retired, one cannot, as a rule, trust their statements or opinions. One settles the question either by collation, by external evidence, by internal evidence, or, in the last, desperate resort, by the intelligent, carefully controlled exercise of that flair without which the delver into the byways of language would do better to refrain from delving at all.

Concerning the aims and methods I pursue in the etymological work in which I am now engaged, I can hardly be expected to speak. But in the introduction to *Name into Word*, I furnish certain clues as to how I went to work on this particular 'sectional' dictionary; in another, *Clichés*, the task was apparently simpler, yet really harder – observation and note-taking over a long period.

The economic problems confronting a professional lexicographer (a lexicographer primarily an author, not a university professor) are much the same as those confronting any other writer, the worst being the precariousness of his livelihood. But whereas a reputable

English novelist has his books manufactured in America, and a reputable American one his in Britain, and thus earns royalties in both countries, a lexicographer has usually to be content, in one of the two countries, with a percentage on the sale of sheets, i.e. with one-quarter to one-third of what the royalties would bring to him. Moreover, like certain other British writers, I had the stocks of several books destroyed during 'the London Blitz'.

And domestic problems? The gravest is the need for quiet in which to concentrate upon work far more exacting than that done by a nominally creative writer. (Lexicography itself can be creative. But that's another story.) Most of the research into written sources, I do in the world's greatest library, that of the British Museum; and my 'field work' - well, naturally that isn't done at home.

Yet, despite all the difficulties, lexicography (except the inferior variety 'cooked up' by hacks) is always fascinating. And often it's fun. Indeed, any fairly well-known writer of readable books on language finds it so. One learns how to 'take it'; from adverse criticism, whether by reviewers or by academics and whether one is at first irritated or amused, one learns, or should learn, more than from favourable comment. The puzzles that arise may, in the attempt to solve them, lead one to discoveries either valuable or entertaining - or both. Etymology, particularly, can be genuinely exciting: a good etymologist, who combines academic learning with human interests, and activity with alertness, might be described as a detective among words, one clue suggesting another, and the second a third, and so on until the quarry is run to earth in Bantu or Basque, in Armorican or Algonquin, in Hittite or Hebrew, in Chinese or Chinook.

Moreover, one's interest is sharpened by correspondents, known or unknown, literate or illiterate, erudite or ignorant, admiring or abusive. Most of them do truly wish to know; many wish to inform; a few – a very few – wish to tell one where one 'gets off'. Now and then, one encounters a most fruitful and learned, courteous and helpful correspondent, and then, as like as not, one gains an amicable assistant. One may even make a friend. The most valued of my collaborators (I've had a hand in several works that benefited by being collaborative) has become a collaborator precisely because he had first been an extremely welcome correspondent, whose worth I immediately perceived. I should have had to be quite unusually stupid, not to perceive it.

Although I have linguistic interests other than lexicography and etymology, and shall, I hope, be able to indulge myself in expressing them, yet, being a passably honest man, I am bound to admit the justice of the charge, 'Once a lexicographer, always a lexicographer'. There are worse fates.

(Written in November, 1950, and published, in a slightly shortened form, in *Tomorrow*, March, 1951.)

THE LANGUAGE OF
CHRISTOPHER FRY

BORN on 18th December, 1907, at Bristol, Christopher Fry went to Bedford Modern School, one of the best in England. On leaving school, he taught and tutored for a year before, in 1927, he became an actor. He then experienced a sad backsliding: for three years he was again a schoolmaster. This experience finally showed him where his talents lay, and he returned to the stage as to a spiritual home. In 1934–36 he directed the Tunbridge Wells Repertory Players. For *She Shall Have Music*, produced in 1935 at the Saville Theatre, London, he wrote both the lyrics and the music. In 1936 he married.

In the following year he wrote *Siege*, a poetic drama not yet performed, not yet published. Now he was fairly launched; almost immediately he wrote *The Boy with a Cart*, which, a short mingling of prose and verse, slightly reminiscent of T. S. Eliot, was performed, rather often, by amateurs and which appeared in print in 1939; it was first acted by professionals only in 1950, at the Lyric Theatre, Hammersmith. Yet 1939 was a fateful year, witnessing the performance, at the Albert Hall, of a pageant play entitled *Thursday's Child* and, at the Tewkesbury Festival, of another such play, *The Tower*; rather incongruously, neither has so far been published. In 1940, he was appointed Director of The Playhouse at Oxford, but in 1941 he enlisted in the Pioneer Corps, with which he served for some four years, fruitful psychologically and spiritually, despite the lack of opportunity to write.

On demobilization, he reverted almost immediately

to the writing of plays, all of them poetic dramas: including *The Firstborn*, published in 1946, *The Lady's Not
for Burning*, 1949, and *Venus Observed* in the following
year.

That sketch needs amplification. *The Boy with a Cart*
is the story of a simple yet compulsive religious faith,
told in neatly dramatic form (for instance, like Eliot
and Auden-Isherwood, Fry arrestingly employs a
modern equivalent of the Greek chorus), couched in
direct, sometimes humorous prose and in well-varied,
often eloquent and always moving verse; with dignity;
upon occasion, with a homely solemnity, yet always
without pomposity; and with a penetrating, amused,
uncomplicated insight into the workings – the strange
impulses and the yet stranger abstentions – of the
human heart. Yet, by the end of 1939, Christopher Fry
was known to few; some of those few, however, sur-
mised a portent and suspected the best. But then, during
a period of six years (1940–45), he did not publish a
single work, and nothing of his was notably performed.
Those six years suddenly yielded the fruit of experience
and meditation. With the publication, 1946, of *The
Firstborn*, he won a respectfully appreciative regard of
certain important literary critics; with its broadcasting,
1947, by the B.B.C., he made the intelligent section of
the general public aware of him; with its performance
at the Edinburgh festival of 1948, he impressed all such
playgoers as had the good fortune to attend. Nor is
this surprising. In *The Firstborn*, set in the Egypt of the
summer of 1200 B.C. (that is, during the oppression of
the Jews by the Pharaoh and at the time of the Plagues),
we see enacted that which, in soberest fact, constitutes
a mighty spiritual drama, more extensive than religion
itself, for it comprehends, under one magnificent can-
opy, a conflict of religion with religion – of race with

race – of mind with mind – also of love with abnega-
tion, and of life with death; the tragedy is related
in language of a sombre splendour; illuminated with
jewelled stars of rhythm and phrasing; in language of
an all-compelling potency. *The Firstborn* possesses a
majestic dignity and a poignant humanity. Theatric-
ally, a great play; poetically, a very great drama.

Likewise published in 1946, but produced a year
earlier (the Mercury Theatre, London, on the 25th of
April, 1946, and revived at the Arts Theatre seven
months later), *A Phoenix too Frequent* affords a startling
contrast with *The Firstborn*. It caused Robert Speaight,
who had starred in T. S. Eliot's *Murder in the Cathedral*
and who is an outstandingly spiritual novelist, to pro-
phesy, after seeing it performed, that 'Mr Fry may
well develop into a really important dramatist' (*Drama
since 1939*, published in 1947). That prophecy came
true, almost exactly two years later. – This *Phoenix*
could not be too frequent. It is a light, dainty, witty
'one-acter'; instinct with life and love and the love of
living, it has a brilliant, mocking cynicism that is only
superficial; Christopher Fry endues the Ephesian
widow of Petronius's gaily heartless story and of some
early 17th Century English dramatist's portrait of a
shallow-pated, fickle girl, with a character warmly
feminine, practical with an expedience tender rather
than repulsive, a character not devoid of depth. With
this coruscating comedy, Fry may fairly be said to have
attained to a delighted recognition by the sophisticated.

In 1948, *Thor, with Angels* was performed in June at
the Canterbury Festival and, to coincide, published in
an acting edition; the first regular edition appeared in
1949. Like *The Boy with a Cart*, this is a religious play,
upon the theme of the coming of Christianity (*with
Angels*) to a man (worshipping *Thor*) and a land, the

G

land recalcitrant, the man reluctant: God o'ermastering them much as Francis Thompson's Christ the fleeing sinner. The grave, stark scene and theme are sweetened with human emotion and with Merlin's introduction of a Celtic beauty and a vatic power. *Thor* has something of the simplicity of *The Boy* and something of the tragic atmosphere of *The Firstborn*: these plays form a dramatic trio of profound religious sentiment, free of sectarianism, proselytising, sanctimony.

In March of that year (1948) he had won general fame; *The Lady's Not for Burning* was produced, on the 10th of the month, at the Arts Theatre. Early in 1949 it was published; and on May 11, it moved to the Globe Theatre, where it met with even better acting and production and with a larger audience. Like *A Phoenix*, *The Lady* is a comedy; but the theme is wider and treated at greater length (a full 'three-acter'); and whereas *A Phoenix* often verges upon farce, *The Lady* occasionally approaches tragi-comedy. Here we have a delectable blend of intellectual and emotional, metaphysical and philological riches: warmth and wit: humour and sharp characterization: caprice, dancing upon a firm foundation: heaven on earth, and earth in heaven: pettiness and triviality, offset by the enduring principle of integrity: the stupid, almost insane blunderings of officialdom, contrasted with an everlasting sanity in those human beings who are unentangled in red tape: lyric refreshment and dramatic zest.

Commissioned by Sir Laurence Olivier, *Venus Observed* was produced, 18 January 1950, at the St James's Theatre, with Sir Laurence in the leading role, that of the Duke of Altair; in February it was published. Whereas *The Lady* was almost entirely vernal, *Venus* is autumnal, yet with spring impinging on the premature resignation of autumn. Closer to comedy than to tragi-comedy, *Venus Observed* stands midway between the debonair lightness and gaiety of *A Phoenix too Frequent* and the full-throated high spirits, blended with a singularly articulate high-mindedness, of *The Lady's Not for Burning*. Beginning with a brief eclipse of the sun and ending with a permanent, though only partial, eclipse of the principal character, it hovers near the precipice of tragedy yet gracefully evades that tragedy. Along with the flowing ease and unforced freshness of *The Lady*, *Venus* displays wit abundantly and, no less abundantly, humour; a deep love of Nature and an even deeper love of human nature. It conveys us upon a breathless visit to the empyrean, yet restores us comfortably to a firm footing on earth. It is at once a wistful elegy to youth unwillingly, wisely forgone, and a lyric to youth that has its own bright-eyed wisdom. And it contains such passages of verse, some surging with impetuous continuity, some sparkling with irrepressible blitheness and some recumbent in mellow ease, as contributed to render *Thor* and *The Lady* likewise unforgettable.

As a pendant to that flashing group of plays, commenced in 1938–39 and completed in 1950 (but merely adumbrating another group – of no less power and, I surmise, yet greater variety), there should be considered *Ring Round the Moon*, Christopher Fry's translation, deft, spirited, elegant, faithful yet reading like an original, of Jean Anouilh's *L'Invitation au château;* a revealing exercise in self-abnegation, which, as ever with the spiritually minded, is also a self-realization. The English version, presented at the Globe Theatre on 26 January, 1950, was published in May. It took much urgent and eloquent persuasion to induce Fry to translate this amusing comedy at all; now he's glad that he did.

Both *Ring Round the Moon* and *The Lady's Not for Burning* were presented in New York during the late autumn of 1950 and early winter of 1950–51: and in the theatres, men listened; when they could not listen, they read. On November 27, 1950, a famous American editor wrote to tell me that Christopher Fry and his work had 'created a good deal of talk in America. Newspapers and magazines have discussed his work at great length' and he added that 'his unusual use of language both puzzles and excites people here'. (It does in Britain too.)

From the November reviews of *The Lady's Not for Burning*, I shall comment, very briefly, upon three, before I try to explain why this English dramatist should have hit America with so sharp an impact. One, bearing the date November 18, has lamentably failed to enter into 'the fun of the thing', charges Fry with being 'the victim of his own uncontrollable fluency' and concludes his remarks upon the plot, thus: 'This is a frail and airy piece of work, but since Mr Fry's intent is clearly literary adornment rather than dramatic activity, it serves its purpose well enough'. With that wrong-headed criticism, penned (I suspect) by one who has never acted in, never directed or produced, never written a play, compare the much-experienced Robert Speaight's description (1946) of Christopher Fry as 'a man of the theatre who is equally prepared for the exigencies of drama and the possibilities of poetry'. *Time*, November 20, in a long article, both biographical and critical, said many worth-while things, and one of the best was this, concerning the first-nighters: 'With a mixture of pleasure and outrage, the audience began to realize that this fellow Fry was breaking all the rules. He was not only pursuing the chancy and self-conscious enterprise' – for Fry, this enterprise is not in the least self-conscious, it being as natural as a minstrel's song, or a lark's – 'of writing verse for the stage; he was writing verse which, like a drink on a hot day or a kiss on a cold night, gave pleasure and satisfaction.' The third is Harold Clurman's notice in *New Republic*, November 27: on the whole, appreciative of the 'literary virtuosity' and the 'bright phrases, happy conceits and a rich heritage of English verse', although he makes too much of the 'verbal sparklers' as opposed to the general excellence of the language; but strangely inappreciative of the dramatic skill and the character-drawing.

From the first and the third of these notices, I should not have deduced either that Fry's language was puzzling and exciting American audiences and readers or that his impact was so widespread and so powerful. Yet, on general principles, that impact and that excited puzzlement can be, at least in part, explained. In *The Lady's Not for Burning*, as in Christopher Fry's other plays, a new world has opened to the New World and has paradoxically, therefore perhaps the more arrestingly, come from the Old, which so many Americans believe to be dead, whereas it's not even moribund: his intense feeling for life – 'the greatest thing in life is life itself' – appeals to those who rightly pride themselves on being alive: in all these plays, the sense of theatre and the dramatic quality, so far from being deficient ('Who on earth would expect good "theatre" in poetic drama?'), are such that they cause many auditors to forget that the vehicle is of verse, not prose, or, if not to forget this inconvenient fact, then to forgive it, – differently phrased, the fusion of poet with playwright is so nearly complete as to be almost indecent: the gripping and the delightful episodes form merely jewels in the crown that is organic architectonics: the freshness of feeling, the vivid approach to the subjects, the immense vitality, have startled a war-weary and blasé world that is so enamoured of sophistication that Fry's lambent sincerity brings a twinge of self-doubting: the brilliant wit that, like Shakespeare's or Sheridan's, does not hold itself superior to the simplicities of a pun, or to the fun of a quibble: the pawky, often gloriously and unashamedly earthy humour, always shrewd, sometimes trenchant, yet never cruel or sadistically malicious, affords refreshment to those (and they are many) who are aweary of the post-1918 world's relentless straining after cleverness: that universality of the treatment which 'makes the whole world kin' – and quite a number of them, brothers and sisters. The universality of the language has implanted a suspicion that, with one or two constructions, several idioms, and a few words changed to accord with American usage, *The Lady's Not for Burning*, or the *Phoenix* or *Thor* or *Venus*, could have been written by an American, if, of course, he had had access to the same crystalline and scintillant spring of poesy. The unconventional dexterity with words naturally appeals to a nation that is dexterous and unconventional with words. The writing of every play has, for Fry, entailed an adventuring and an adventure; and this spirit of joyous enterprise results in the auditor or the reader becoming involved in the same felicitous chain of events. Not only is there a liberation of the English language, there is also a liberation of the British spirit, with the result that those Americans who are of British descent and yet do not feel constrained to deny it find themselves liberated, both in language and in mind and spirit. Then, too, numerous Americans have, I think, perceived that here is one who, like so many of their countrymen (and women), doesn't give a damn or care a hoot for anybody, yet cares a very great deal for everybody: his quiet, modest, unmistakable independence and self-reliance have been discerned by Americans, who make a cult of sturdy independence. It is extremely difficult, whether one is American or British, to prevent oneself from being impressed and delighted by the work of this born playwright (defiant of petty rules and cramping conventions) and born poet (now Elizabethan, now Augustan, now 20th Century) employing a medium that had, somewhat prematurely, been presumed dead; one who, even while he was setting them in an historical period and, rather nonchalantly, tying them, here and there, to history, invested his characters and his language, hence the plays as entities, with a timelessness that has lulled many an auditor, not a few readers, into a comfortable indifference to strict historical accuracy and into a ready acceptance of Fry's non-acceptance of limitations either chronological or racial.

Perhaps, too, Fry's philosophy of life, in so far as it has been implied (he never preaches) in his plays, has struck a responsive chord in a considerable number of American hearts. Numerous passages in *The Firstborn*, in *The Lady's Not for Burning* and in *Venus Observed* indicate, rather than obtrude, the nature of that philosophy, yet none so clearly as in Jennet's declaration in the third act of *The Lady*:

> I seem to wish to have some importance
> In the play of time. If not,
> Then sad was my mother's pain, sad my breath,
> Sad the articulation of my bones,
> Sad, sad my alacritous web of nerves,
> Woefully, woefully sad my wondering brain,
> To be shaped and sharpened into such tendrils
> Of anticipation, to feed the swamp of space.
> What is deep, as love is deep, I'll have

Deeply. What is good, as love is good,
I'll have well. Then if time and space
Have any purpose, I shall belong to it.
If not, if all is a pretty fiction
To distract the cherubim and seraphim
Who so continually do cry, the least
I can do is to fill the curled shell of the world
With human deep-sea sound, and hold it to
The ear of God, until he has appetite
To taste our salt sorrow on his lips.*

This philosophy can be seen to inform all his writing.
The language in general and the style in particular, are,
moreover, as they are, because *that*, precisely *that*, is
what the various characters are trying to say: not what
the poet wishes them to say, but what they themselves,
being truly themselves, would say.

That philosophy and that faithfulness to character
largely determine the metric, the occasional use of
prose, and the incidence of rhyme and assonance. Even
the prosy talk of the neighbours in *The Boy* exemplifies
his rhyming skill:

One after the other we have gone indoors
Turning it over in our minds as we went
About our chores. What will the old woman do,
Dear heart, with no roof over her head, no man,
No money, and her boy doing nothing
But make a cart?

'I will tell you some other time,' he said.
'I am in a hurry.' Well, that's his look-out
It's not for us to worry.

* The author wishes to thank both Mr Fry for his gracious
permission to quote freely from his works and the Oxford University Press and, for *The Boy with a Cart*, Messrs Frederick Muller,
Ltd, for their equally generous corroboration of that permission.

Apparently rhymeless, those two stanzas contain the artfully contrived *indoors—chores, heart—cart, hurry—worry.* Fry's metric is varied and subtle and almost incredibly dexterous. Passages more nobly beautiful could be quoted from *The Firstborn*, Merlin's long speech ('Welcome, sleep') in *Thor* has greater poetic merit and diversity, several in *The Lady* breathe a more humoursome humanity; yet for sheer brilliance and breath-taking fluency of versification, combined with pellucidity of meaning, the following lines, spoken by Perpetua in *Venus Observed*; lines swift yet smooth, magical yet rich in good-sense, heart-warm—yet head-cool, lines that throw as much light upon the poet's extraordinary command of language as upon the deft certainty of his metric; could hardly be bettered:

> There isn't any reason
> Why a sentence, I suppose, once it begins,
> Once it has risen to the lips at all
> And finds itself happily wandering
> Through shady vowels and over consonants
> Where ink's been spilt like rivers or like blood
> Flowing for the cause of some half-truth
> Or a dogma now outmoded, shouldn't go
> Endlessly moving in grave periphrasis
> And phrase in linking phrase, with commas falling
> As airily as lime flowers, intermittently,
> Uninterrupting, scarcely troubling
> The mild and fragile progress of the sense
> Which trills trebling like a pebbled stream
> Or lowers towards an oath-intoning ocean
> Or with a careless and forgetful music
> Looping and threading, tuning and entwining,
> Flings a bable of bells, a carolling
> Of such various vowels the ear can almost feel
> The soul of sound when it lay in chaos yearning
> For the tongue to be created: such a hymn

If not as lovely, then as interminable,
As restless, and as heartless, as the hymn
Which in the tower of heaven the muted spheres
With every rippling heart and windy horn
Played for incidental harmony
Over the mouldering rafters of the world,
Rafters which seldom care to ring, preferring
The functional death-watch beetle, stark, staccato,
Economical as a knuckle-bone,
Strict, correct, but undelighting
Like a cleric jigging in the saturnalia,
The saturnalia we all must keep,
Green-growing and rash with life,
Our milchy, mortal, auroral, jovial,
Harsh, unedifying world,
Where every circle of grass can show a dragon
And every pool's as populous as Penge,
Where birds, with taffeta flying, scarf the air
On autumn evenings, and a sentence once
Begun goes on and on, there being no reason
To draw to any conclusion so long as breath
Shall last, except that breath
Can't last much longer.

By implication, something has already been said
about the language employed by Christopher Fry in
his poetic dramas. Only a few other aspects remain to
be considered, one of the most important being the
charge, often laid against him, of anachronism. To
take only one play, I have noted in *The Lady* the
following potential candidates: *barracking*, in 'I ask nothing, nothing. Stop Barracking my heart'; *bash*, in
'Whatever happens I shall have one bash at him';
blastoderm, in 'O blastoderm of injustice, You multipli-
cation of double crossing!'; *boomerang*, in 'boomerang
rages and lunacies'; *graft*, in 'She has bribed you to pro-
cure Her death! Graft! Graft!'; *pipsqueak*, in 'You crapu-

lous puddering pipsqueak!'; *thrombosis;* and 'With sufficient organ-music, sadly sent out On the wrong wave
of sound'.

An error in the order of time, especially the placing
of an event too early, anachronism is primarily a matter
of history and the concern of historians. In *The Lady,*
set in the year '1400 either more or less or exactly'
(could there be a neater, sweeter mockery of pedants?),
the only possible charges of historical error are against
the use of *boomerang,* Australia being discovered several
centuries later – but the poet is using *boomerang* as an
adjective, without reference to the weapon; and against
'sent out On the wrong wave of sound' – with its merely
apparent reference to wireless telegraphy and its real
allusion to the ancient 'music of the spheres', an allusion
made the more arresting to the audiences of 1949–51
by the apparent reference. Every other term in the preceding paragraph refers to an act, a person, a physio-
logical or medical fact, as common, as prevalent, in
1400 as in 1950. To say that *barracking* and *bash* are
modern slang, or that such technicalities as *blastoderm*
and *thrombosis* did not exist in 1400, is, so far as anachronism is concerned, to convict oneself of a quite
remarkable stupidity, for, in this respect, all language
current in the mid-20th Century is anachronistic for
characters supposed to be speaking in 1400: in this
sense, all language whatsoever is 'anachronistic'. In
fact, there is no such thing as linguistic anachronism,
there is only historical anachronism: almost every
charge of anachronism springs from an ignorance no
less remarkable than the stupidity. To complain that
the language seems to be unnecessarily or blatantly
modernistic is one thing, springing from a dislike of
modernism or from a fear of the contemporary. As
applied to Fry, these charges of anachronism are, to put

it courteously, sheer 'hooey'; indeed, it's high time someone 'blew the gaff' on the entire question of literary anachronism and exposed it for the rank nonsense and muddled thinking (if you can call it thinking) it so clearly is.

To pass to a positive quality. The plays abound in speeches, lines, phrases of memorable beauty, not only of content but also of sound. 'Musical loveliness' marks such passages as these, chosen from *The Firstborn*:

> . . . the smooth endless
> Music of the Nile.—
> . . . this land of cities
> Lying dazed with time's faithfulness.

But it is more logical, more sensible, to speak of the magnificent imagery, exemplified in the same play:

> Egypt is only
> One golden eruption of time, one flying spark
> Attempting the ultimate fire.—

> God will unfasten the hawk of death from his
> Grave wrist, to let it rake our world,
> Descend and obliterate the firstborn of Egypt,
> All the firstborn, cattle, flocks and men:
> Mortality lunging in the midnight fields
> And briding in the beds.—

> With prayers like the grip of a moon
> On the long tide of her caravan.—

> Love is the dominant of life, to which all our changes
> Of key are subdued in the end. You will be able
> To wander the winding and coïtous passages
> Of the heart.—

> The bewildering mesh of God.

The imagery, even the metaphors at their most luxuriant, are seen to be firmly controlled, as, for instance, are these from *Venus Observed*:

> We 're here this morning to watch
> The sun annulled and renewed, and to sit affectionately
> Over the year's dilapidation.—

> . . . never speak
> Of the climate of Eden, or the really magnificent
> Foliage of the tree of knowledge,
> Or the unforgettable hushed emerald
> Of the coiling and fettering serpent.—

> The floor is battering at your feet like Attila
> With a horde of corybantic atoms.

Sometimes the metaphor or the simile is vivid, sharp, tangy, as in

> Watching the herons . . .
> They haunt the dregs of the mist like ghosts
> Left on the yellow morning by a tide of sleep. (*Thor.*)

More often, however, we are struck with the loveliness, as in these verses from *A Phoenix Too Frequent:*

> A mystery 's in the world
> Where a little liquid, with flavour, quality and fume
> Can be as no other, can hint and flute our senses
> As though a music played in harvest hollows
> And a movement was in the swathes of memory.—

> It 's morning; I see a thin dust of daylight
> Blowing on to the steps.—

> How did it come
> Our stars could mingle for an afternoon
> So long ago, and then . . .
> . . . helplessly look on the dark high seas
> Of our separation, while time drank
> The golden hours? What hesitant fate is that?

(Contrasting other women to the belovèd, Tegeu
speaks of)

>   Stars lost and uncertain
> In the sea, compared with the shining salt, the shiners,
> The galaxies, the clusters, the bright grain whirling
> Over the black threshing-floor of space.

Fry displays a mastery – rarely equalled – of the
organic simile, audacious, self-contained, poetical, as in
Venus Observed, where the middle-aged Duke alleges as
a reason for marriage:

>   Why? Because I see no end
> To the parcelling out of heaven in small beauties,
> Year after year, flocks of girls, who look
> So lately kissed by God
> They come out on the world with lips shining,
> Flocks and generations, until time
> Seems like nothing so much
> As a blinding snowstorm of virginity,
> And a man, lost in the perpetual scurry of white,
> Can only close his eyes
> In a resignation of monogamy.—
>
> And I, as unlaborious
> As a laburnum tree, hang in caresses of gold.
>
>   To-night will go past, as a swan
> Will pass like a recurring dream
> On the light sleep of the lake,
> And I shall be smoothed away in the wake of the swan.

To speak of imagery is perhaps unfairly to diminish
the spacious breadth and beauty, the power and preg-
nancy, of the language. Consider the slowly mounting
poetic eloquence of

> What I'm inflicted with
> Is strong, destroying me with a cry of love,
> A violence of humility arrogantly
> Demanding all I am or possess or have ambitions for,
> Insistent as a tocsin which was sounded
> When the sun first caught on fire, and ever since
> Clangs alarm with a steady beat in the wild
> Night of history.

Facility in the use of vivid figures of speech merges into the broader considerations of poetic power – and of an unashamed delight in language. The only reason why certain critics sneer at Christopher Fry's evident – or rather, avowed – delight in language is that they lack the power. Did Shakespeare curb his delight in the exercise of his rare power over language? Has any other poet worthy of the name curbed it? What curbs one is the expressing of that delight. Examine the contrasted manners of these two passages from *Venus Observed*, the one quiet, the other rumbustious:

> She and I, sharing two solitudes,
> Will bear our spirits up to where not even
> The nightingale can know,
> Where the song is quiet, and quiet
> Is the song.—

> You're a vain, vexing, incomprehensible,
> Crimping, constipated duffer. What's your heart?
> All plum duff! Why do I have to be
> So inarticulate? God give me a few
> Lithontriptical words! You grovelling little
> Gobemouche! ....
> You spigoted, bigoted, operculated prig!

The latter passage is, in its manner, reminiscent of the joyous word-flinging of the Elizabethans and of certain Jacobean and Caroline dramatists. Incidentally,

it is precisely this early 17th Century trait which has,
especially in New York, exasperated and been grossly
misunderstood by those conventionals for whom Mar-
lowe, Shakespeare, Ben Jonson and James Joyce might
just as well not have got themselves born.   Two passages selected from *The Lady* for impatient (and imperceptive) reprehension have been these:

> You babble-mouthing, fog-blathering,
> Chin-chuntering, chap-flapping, liturgical,
> Turgidical, base old man! –
> The whole thing's a lot of amphigenious,
> Stultiloquential fiddle-faddle.

Admittedly, one would soon weary of that sort of
thing – if there were much of it. Only very rarely has
Fry carried it too far; even then, only by a phrase or
two or, at most, a line or two.

Also reminiscent – although in inspiration quite independent – of those dramatists, are the moonlit poetry,
the noonday richness, of

> Ramases,
> She has come so gifted for you, possessing
> A fable of rubies, and pearls like seeds of the moon
> With metal and strange horns, ebon and ivory,
> Spilling chalcedonyx and male sapphires.
> .... Do they glimmer
> Nowhere in the cupboards of your sleep?
>
> (*The Firstborn*)

That, in a few speeches of the comedies, there is an
element of preciosity, of rarefaction and alembication,
no sane critic would deny. In *The Boy*, *The Firstborn*
and *Thor*, this element occurs hardly at all. Fry's poetry
coruscates and scintillates: the gleam and the glister
have blinded the mediocre to his immense talent and

to his probably considerable genius. His head is among the stars (no bad place for a poet's, indeed any writer's head, to be); his feet, firmly, comfortably, laughingly treading the soil he loves. The mediocre, forgetting his vigour, his unquestionable adequacy to any, to every, theme, his humour, his gallant epigrams, forget also the quiet strength and the seasonal yet sempiternal rightness and beauty of his country scenes. Love of the country engarlands his imagery with a delicate, precise realism – rather like that which we encounter in the best work of Edmund Blunden and Geoffrey Grigson – as in this description of the coming of rain to a drought-dry land in *The Boy with a Cart*:

> We saw the little tempest in the grass,
> The panic of anticipation: heard
> The uneasy leaves flutter, the air pass
> In a wave, the fluster of the vegetation;
>
> Heard the first spatter of drops, the outriders
> Larruping up the road, hitting against
> The gate of the drought, and shattering
> On to the lances of the tottering meadow.

And in these two passages from *Thor, with Angels*:

> I can hear
> Faintly on the twittering sea a sail
> Moving greatly where the waves, like harvest-home,
> Come hugely on our coast: the men of Rome
> Returning, bringing God, winter over, a breath
> Of green exhaled from the hedges, the wall of sky
> Breached by larksong. Primrose and violet
> And all frail privileges of the early ground
> Gather like pilgrims in the aisles of the sun.
> A ship in full foliage rides in
> Over the February foam, and rests
> Upon Britain.—

H

                                    I know well enough
The weight of the silence that's on our shoulders now.
I move under it like the moving mole
That raises the hackles of dead leaves.

The final impression one gains after a careful consideration and a scrupulous examination of the printed
plays is that, for all his brilliance and high spirits, for
all his mockery and witticisms, for all his verbal ex-
travagances, for all his modernity, Christopher Fry has
achieved such a body of work in the poetic drama as
overtops that of any poet since the 17th Century. More
important than the profusion and the fluency, is the
underlying, profound seriousness of purpose. Like
Donne, he is a metaphysical; like Donne, he is spiritual.
His dramas are, above all, spiritual rather than metaphysical: yet, unlike many spiritual writers, he realizes
that the spirit works in and upon the body as well as
with and upon mind; he also realizes that the emotions
have a beauty – yes, and a logic – of their own. His
aim, as I see it, is to write, and cause to be performed,
plays that shall constitute a poetic and convincing
presentation of the vast, never-ending drama implicit
in the establishment, and then the maintenance, of
truth; a presentation also of those problems which are
implicit in the attainment and preservation of freedom,
whether spiritual or intellectual or physical, whether
collective (that is, political) or individual (that is, personal): but he has effected all this without the stifling
paraphernalia of solemnity, without the cramping
pusillanimities of officialdom, and without recourse to
formal religion: with, however, recourse to informal
religion – the inner light – and with an invincible faith
in the worth of human nature.
And he has done it by means of language that is
fresh, vivid, alert; fluent, because unforced; brilliant,

many-faceted; infinitely adaptable and various; usually direct and always sincere; drawing, for its strength, upon life and prose, and for its beauty, upon contemplation, ecstasy and poetry.

(Written during the last fortnight of 1950 and revised during the first of 1951, this article appeared in *Tomorrow*, July, 1951, in a slightly different form: there, the quotations from *The Boy with a Cart* were lacking, as were the references to the English version of the Greek chorus and those to Edmund Blunden and Geoffrey Grigson; there, too, the theme of Elizabethan word-flinging was mentioned only in one brief sentence, without the two short quotations from *The Lady's Not for Burning*. – There, a personal note preceded the essay; here, its presence would not be entirely felicitous, and I have decided to omit it.)

Postscript (3 June 1951). On May 31, Christopher Fry's spiritual drama *A Sleep of Prisoners* was published, some six weeks after the first performance. As a play, it is infinitely moving: it affords a tremendous spiritual experience.

As written drama, *A Sleep of Prisoners* fascinates the student of language. With its familiar turns of speech, its linking of stark fact to singularly significant nightmare, its marriage of story and allegory, of realism and symbolism, its immediacy and simplicity of phrasing, *A Sleep* goes beyond even *The Boy with a Cart* in directness of style: and yet it contains much notable poetry. Or rather, the poetry is always notable, for the dramatist employs an arrestingly modern idiom with such felicity that only in reading does one think of this as a poetic drama; hearing it, one rarely, or never, thinks of the medium at all, except perhaps in one or two of Peter's more lyrical speeches. Although it possesses stylistic elements, the language is sometimes common-

place, yet, as a whole, the language is brilliantly successful; in the context, indeed, none of it is commonplace –
and outside of context, language, as distinct from words,
does not exist.

To say that *A Sleep of Prisoners* is intensely spiritual
either despite or even because of the language would
be to mistake the intention and the method. Christopher
Fry has achieved his intention by an inconspicuous yet
masterly fusion of matter and manner. In short, he is
a great writer.

ARTICLED NOUNS

THERE are numerous nouns consisting of either the
definite article (English *the*, Arabic *al*, French *le* or *la* or
l', Spanish *el* or *la*, Italian *la*) or the English indefinite
article *an*, prefixed to another word, usually a noun,
and thus forming a new noun. In formation they
are comparable to *naunt*, from *mine aunt* and *thine aunt*,
and *nuncle*, from *mine uncle* and *thine uncle*. For the
English *an*, there are alternative processes, which will
duly be considered.

ENGLISH

The English definite article *the* combining with a noun
is exemplified in *nonce*, occurring in the phrase *for the
nonce*, deriving from Middle English *for the nones*, from
for then ones, the n of *then* being a survival of Old English
m in *tham*, dative of the article *the*, and *ones* being an
adverb from *one*, one.

The indefinite *an* sometimes combines with a noun
beginning with a vowel to form a new noun – beginning
with *n*. The M.E. *an ekename*, literally 'an addition(al)
name', was misapprehended as *a nekename*: hence *a nickname*: hence the now independent *nickname*. The M.E.
newte, whence the modern *newt*, arose from the incorrect division of *an ewte* as *a newte*; *ewte* or *evete* derived
from O.E. *efete*, lizard, whence also the zoological *eft*;
O.E. *efete* is of obscure origin. The dialectal *hickwall*
or green woodpecker, 'formerly also *hyghwhele*, *highawe*,
perhaps of imitative origin' (Webster), has a variant
ickle, now usually *nickle*, *an ickle* becoming *a nickle*. The
American localism *nimshi*, a fool, derives from the

103

Suffolk-dialectal *nimshi(e)*, a flighty girl: and *nimshie* derives from *a nimshie*, incorrect division of *an imshie*; *imshie* derives from the mainly Scottish *hims*, flighty, half-witted, itself from Old Norse *heimskr*, foolish – compare Old High German *heimisc*, home-keeping, hence 'simple' – from O.N. *heima*, home. That homely word *ninny* seems to have been torn from *a ninny*, apparently from *an innocent*: in *an inno*(cent), the *o* is, when slurred in conversation, yet another instance of 'the neutral vowel', every *ă*, *ĕ*, *ĭ*, *ŏ*, *ŭ*, being 'neutral' or indeterminate in rapid, rather careless pronunciation – short *a, i, o, u* becoming (almost) indistinguishable from short *e*. Yet another instance of 'foolish *n*' occurs in the obsolete *nidiot* – *an idiot* being read as *a nidiot* – and in its derivative, the archaic *nidget*, a word clearly occasioned by slovenly pronunciation. The English and Scottish dialectal *nope* derives from *a nope*, incorrect division of *an ope*: and *ope* is merely a dialectal variant of *alp*, a bullfinch; *alp* is of unknown origin. Compare *notch*, from *a notch*, probably an incorrect division of *an otch*: *otch* derives from M.E. *oche*, itself from Old French *osche* (Modern *hoche*), perhaps from Old Fr. *oschier*, to nick or notch, although at least one authority prefers to draw the verb from the noun, which he declares to be of unknown origin.

The reverse process occurs in, e.g., *adder, apron, orange, umpire*, where the *n-* of the noun becomes the *-n* of *an*. Thus *adder* is independent for *an adder*, originally incorrect for *a nadder*. True, late Middle English already has *addre*: but *addre* is independent for *a naddre*: and *naddre* or *neddre* derives from O.E. *nǣdre*, a snake, especially an adder. With *nǣdre* compare Old Saxon *nādra*, Gothic *nadrs*, O.H.G. *nātara* or *nātr* (cf. German *Natter* and Old Irish *nathir*) and, earlier, the Latin *natrix*, a water snake. Although *natrix* probably does not come from L. *natare*, to swim, the 'water' specialization may, in popular etymology, have been influenced by *natare*.

Other instances of this sort of formation by incorrect division are as follows: –

Aitchbone (folk-etymologized to *edgebone*): *an aitchbone*: *a nachebone*, the M.E. *nache* or *nage* being adopted from Old Fr. *nache* or *nage*, itself from an assumed Low Latin *natica*, popular variant of L. *natis*, a buttock, of which the plural *nates* is used in anatomy and zoology; *natis* may be akin to Greek *nōtos*, the back, perhaps also to Sanskrit *nitambaḥ*, buttocks. The English *natch* or rump (especially of cattle) comes straight from Old Fr. *nache*.

Apron: *an apron*, incorrect division of M.E. *a napron*: *napron*, from Old Fr. *naperon*, diminutive of *nape* (Modern Fr. *nappe*), itself from L. *mappa*, a (table) napkin.

Auger: *an auger*, incorrect (already in M.E.) for *a nauger*: *nauger* (retained in dialect, from O.E. *nafugār*; i.e., *nafu*, nave of a wheel + *gār*, a spear: literally, therefore, *nafugār* was a 'nave-borer'.

Eyas, falconers' 'hawk taken from the nest' and ordinary men's 'nestling, fledgling': *an eyas*: *a nias* or *a nyas* (obsolete for 'young hawk; hence, unsophisticated person'): Fr. *niais*, fresh from the nest: assumed Low L. *nidax*: L. *nidus*, a nest.

Orange: Old Fr. *orenge*: Portuguese *auranja*, influenced by Port. *aur* (from L. *aurum*), gold: earlier Port. *aranja*; earlier still, *naranja*, the *n-* getting itself lost by confusion with the preceding indefinite article, *una* (feminine): Arabic *nāranj*: Persian *nārang*: Sanskrit *nāranga*: a stem meaning 'fragrant' (cf. Tamil *naru*, fragrant). Despite the fact that, in English, there has probably been no *a n-*confusion, *orange* figures here because of its fundamental relevance and because of the two related terms *aurantium* and *naringin*. The Sanskrit *nāranga* has a variant *nārangī*, whence Marathi *nāringī*, orange, whence *naringin*, a glucoside found in the blossoms and fruit of the grapefruit. From the Port. *auranja* (see above), an orange, botanists formed, with a Latin *-tium* ending, the word *aurantium*, for such fruits as the orange.

Umbles is perhaps an example, for of the forms *numbles, umbles, humbles*, the third seems to be a late variation (influenced by the adjective *humble*, originally pronounced *umble*) of *umbles*: and *umbles* is later than *numbles*: apparently *a numbles* became *an umbles*.

Umpire: *an umpire*: *a numpire*: *numpire*, from M.E. *nompere* or *nounpere*, from Old Fr. *nomper*, *nonper*: *non*, not + *per* (Modern *pair*), equal (compare L. *impar*, unequal, uneven). The *umpire* is an 'uneven', i.e. a third, party or person.

SPANISH

The Spanish definite article – *el* (masculine) and *la* (feminine) – occurs in a few words. The most obvious is *eldorado*, coalescing *el dorado*, the gilded (hence, the golden) – hence, any place or region fabulously rich. *Larigo*, in Spanish American horsemanship, appears to result, by dropping the *e-*, from Sp. *el arraigo*, the firmly-fixed. The best example of *el* incorporated is formed by *alligator*: Sp. *el lagarto*, the lizard, via *el lagarto de Indias*, the (aquatic) lizard of the Indies, the (American) crocodile.

The Spanish feminine 'the' – i.e., *la* – occurs most notably in *lagniappe* and *lariat*. The latter merely combines *la*, the, with *reata*, a rope. Originally, *la reata* was 'the (thing) tied' – *reata* being the feminine of *reato*, past participle of the verb *reatar*.

Lagniappe, however, differs from *lariat*, for whereas the latter is 'pure' Spanish, the former is 'impure'. The

story of *lagniappe*, a small present, in kind, from a tradesman to a customer, has been told best by Horace
Reynolds in his delightful article, 'The South Has Three
Words for It' – in *The Christian Science Monitor* of 28 April
1950. 'Like *chocolate, maize, potato, savannah,* and *tomato*,
it is a word which has come into English from the
American Indian through the Spanish. . . . The Incas
had the pleasant custom of lagniappe and a word for
it – *yapa*'; Quechuan, their language, shows the variant
yapani.* 'The Spaniards took the word over from the
Incas' and pronounced it at first *yapa*, then *ñapa*. 'It
traveled to New Orleans with the Spaniards' and there
'the French Creoles gallicized it into *lagniappe*, putting
the French definite article *la* before the Spanish *ñapa*' –
probably because the custom of *ñapa* was always spoken
of as *la ñapa*. 'In that state, Mark Twain found it and
gave it currency in American.' Rather, he popularized
it in 1863; *A Dictionary of American English* records it
for 1849. The other two words, by the way, are *brotus*,
perhaps – as Reynolds suggests – akin to English dialectal *brot*, or *brott*, a small quantity, and *brotta*, a small
quantity, especially a little in addition, but more probably a lopped (and then corrupted) form of Spanish
albricias, a gratuity (see *albricias* in the 'Amenities' group
of the Arabic section); and *pilon* (pronounced *pilōn*), the
Spanish *pilón*, a cone-shaped cake of sugar.

FRENCH

The French definite article, *le* (masculine) or *la* (feminine) or *l'* (whether *le* or *la*) before a vowel, appears
almost too obviously in *lacrosse*, the (*la*) hooked stick

* Augusto Malaret, *Diccionario de Americanismos*, 3rd edition –
not dated, but ca. 1947. Mexican Spanish still uses *yapa*: Mafer,
Diccionario Mexico, 1946.

(*crosse*: English *cross*); in *lapeyrousia* or *lapeirousia*, a South African iris named after Jean, comte de *la Peyrouse* or *la Pérouse* (1741–88), a French naval officer; and in *lavallière*, usually written *lavaliere* or *lavalier*, from Fr. *la vallière* or *lavallière*, perhaps from Louise de *La Vallière*, one of the more enduring rays of sunshine that illuminated the life of 'Le Roi-Soleil'.

Very much less obvious are *ammunition*, exemplifying one process, and *lage*, *lammer*, *lingot*, *lisle*, *loriot*, exemplifying the opposite process. *Ammunition* slightly adapts the Fr. *amunition*, a term formerly used for *munition* and arising from a misapprehension of *la munition* as *l'amunition*. *Lage*, water, urine, and *lag*, a washing (only in *lag of duds*), are underworld variants of a word that represents 12th–14th Century Fr. *l'aige* or, rather, *l'aigue*, (the) water. The Scottish, and Northern English, *lammer*, amber, is a slovening of Fr. *l'ambre*, the amber. *Lingot*, an ingot or the mould in which it is made, constitutes an English adoption of Fr. *lingot*, itself a misapprehension of Fr. *l'ingot*, 'the ingot', *ingot* – literally 'the in-poured' – being a thoroughly English term, borrowed by French. Moreover, Fr. *lingot* probably accounts for the otherwise obscure weaving term, *lingo* (unpronounced Fr. *t* being dropped) or *lingoe* (a further anglicization), a piece of lead used as a weight. *Lisle* is short for *lisle thread*, thread originally made at *Lisle*, the former spelling of the famous manufacturing city of *Lille*, situated on the river Deule – hence its name, *l'isle* (modern *l'île*), the island. *Loriot* comes straight from French, where it represents an alteration of *loriol*, itself a coalescence of *l'oriol*.

Then there is the combination of preposition + definite article + noun, as in *Algernon*: *al gernon*: wherein *al* fuses *a* (modern *à*), with *le*, the, and *gernon* (or *gernun* – both being, by metathesis, for *grenon*) means 'mous-

tache': 'He of the (presumably notable) moustache'.
And *grenon* derives from a Common Teutonic *grani*,
akin to Latin *crines*, collectively 'hair of the head'.

ITALIAN

The same combination – preposition + definite article
+ noun – occurs in certain words drawn from Italian.
Typical are *alarm, alert, aligreek*. The verb *alarm* derives
from the noun *alarm*, of which *alarum* (M.E. *alarom*)
merely shows a rolled *r*: and an *alarm*, M.E. *alarme*, has
been adopted from French, which thus adapted It.
all'arme, to the arms: *all'* = *alle*, to the (feminine plural);
and *arme*, arms = the plural of *arma*, feminine, from
the Latin plural *arma*, arms, weapons, apprehended
as a singular. As Italian *all'arme* was a warning cry
('to arms!'), so It. *all'erta* meant 'on the watch', literally
'on the watch-tower' or 'on the height': *all'* = *a*, on,
at + *la*, the (feminine) + *erta*, a slope, a look-out, from
erto, steep, originally the past participle of *ergere*, short
for *erigere*, from L. *erigere*, to erect. The It. *all'erta*, like
a number of other Italian military terms, passed into
French; as *a l'erte*, which became the adjective *alerte*,
which became the English *alert* – whence the noun,
whence the verb. Likewise, It. *alla greca*, in the Greek
(manner, *maniera* or *guisa*), became the English archi-
tectural *aligreek*, a Greek fret. A simpler combination
occurs in the old dance known as *lavolta*, which combines *la*, the, and *volta*, a whirl or whirling.

DUTCH

The Dutch *de*, the, occurs certainly in one English
word, *daffodil*, and probably in another, *decoy*. The verb
'to *decoy*' comes straight from the noun: and in the

noun *decoy* the element *coy* represents the Dutch *koit*, a
cage; *koit* and *cage*, in fact, derive from a common stem.
The element *de* appears to be the Dutch article *de*, and
the English word as a whole, the Dutch *de koit*. A *decoy*
is primarily a cage or trap for wild fowl. *Daffodil* con-
flates the Dutch *de affodil*, the affodil or affodill; *affodil*
reshapes the Old French *afrodille*, a 'mutilation' of
Latin *asphodelus*, a transliteration of Greek *asphodelos*.
(*Affodill*, by the way, is obsolete; it comes from the
Medieval Latin *affodillus*, a softening of L. *asphodelus*.)
The Gr. *asphodelos*, ἀσφόδελος, is of uncertain origin: that
brilliant scholar, the late Emile Boisacq of Brussels,
essays no etymology of his own and tepidly mentions
another scholar's suggestion that the Greek word derives
from an Indo-European stem bearing the basic sense
'trembling'.

ARABIC *

Certain English derivatives from Arabic *al*, the, combined with an Arabic noun, are 'disguised'. A fairly
comprehensive list could be formed by checking the
terms assembled by Walt Taylor in his instructive
Arabic Words in English (S.P.E. tract, No. 38), published
in 1933; I have aimed to be merely representative. For
orcanet, see *alkanet* – five paragraphs inward. *Lute* has
passed from Old Fr. *leut* (Modern *luth*), altered from
Provençal *laüt*, which, in transliterating the Arabic
al-ʿcud, the piece of wood, drops the *a-* and narrows
'piece of wood' to 'such a piece of wood as is used in
building the instrument'. In one sense (for they begin
with *a-*) more deceptive, are *acton, apricot, artichoke,
azarole, azimene, azimuth* and *azoth*. In the Middle Ages,
acton denoted a stuffed jacket worn under mail armour:

* For certain Arabic words, I have to thank the late Gerald
Hatchman for some illuminating assistance.

M.E. *acton*: Old Fr. *aketon* (or *auqueton*), a quilted jacket: Spanish *alcotón*, *algodón*, cotton: Arabic *al-quṭn* or *al-quṭun*, the cotton. Note that *algodón* appears in a few dictionaries of English, the term being common in Spanish America; note also that *cotton*, M.E. *coton*, Old Fr. *coton*, Sp. *cotón*, Ar. *quṭn* or *quṭun*, has dropped the *al*. Like *alcohol-kohl*, *alcoran-koran*, *alcayde-cadi*, *alguazil-vizier*, the pair *algodón-cotton* exemplifies the early (or *al*-) and the late borrowings. Most of the derivatives from *cotton* – for instance, *cottonseed*, *cottonwood*, *cottony*, even *cottonade* – are straightforward; the verbs *cotton*, to make friends, get along well together, and *cotton to*, to become attached to or fond of, arise from the fact that cotton tends to cling or stick. Also to the vegetable world belong *apricot* and *artichoke*, much-travelled words for much-travelled things, and the less famous *azarole*. *Apricot* constitutes an English 'easement' of Fr. *abricot*, earlier *aubercot*, a reshaping of Portuguese *albricoque*, an adaptation of Arabic *al-burquq*, itself – the article apart – an adaptation of Late Greek *praikokion*, from Latin *praecoquum*, the neuter of the adjective *praecoquus*, variant of *praecox*, early ripe, *praecoquum* being used as a noun to designate, at first, an early-ripe peach; *apricot*, therefore, is linked to *precocious*. *Artichoke* derives from the Italian *articiocco*, which, like the Sp. *alcachofa*, the Port. *alcachofra* and the Fr. *artichaut* (via Lombard *articoic*, a distortion of Fr. *carciofo*, short for It. *archicioffo*, parallel to *archiciocco*, a form earlier than *articiocco*), derives from Arabic *al-khurshūf*, the artichoke; *al-khurshūf* is generic for *khurshūf*, artichoke. Ivor Brown, in *Having the Last Word*, 1950, illuminatingly cites a quatrain from Edward FitzGerald's *Rubaiyat of Omar Khayyam*:

And evermore I went, alone, aloof,
Beneath the blazing Heaven's burnish'd Roof

To drink the Vine of Solitude and seek
The Peace that's rooted strong as Al-Kharshuf.

The shrub *azarole*, growing an agreeable fruit, has derived its name from French *azarole* (later *azerole*),
borrowed from Spanish *acerola*, an adaptation of Arabic
al-zuʿrūr, the azarole – generic, like *al-khurshūf* above and
al-zāwūq below. Passing to science, we have the astrolo-
gical *azimene* and the *azimuth* and the alchemical *azoth*.
Azimene, of obscure origin, probably comes from Arabic
al-zamānah, the evil affection; *azimuth* via Fr. *azimut*,
from Ar. *al-sumūt*, plural of *al-samt*, the way or direction,
hence the arc. Mercury or *azoth*, regarded by the alchemists as the first principle of metals, hence its adoption by Paracelsus for his universal remedy, hence
(*Azoth*) a potent spirit dwelling in a talismanic jewel of
Paracelsus's, – *azoth* represents Arabic *al-zāwūq*, the
quicksilver; *al-zāwūq*, like *al-khurshūf* above, is obviously
generic. In several words, the change springs from the
pronunciation of Arabic *al* as *el* – as it tends to be pronounced in Egypt. The best example is *elixir*, adopted
from Medieval Latin, which thus deformed the Ar.
al-iksīr, the medicinal powder (*par excellence*); *iksīr* is an
alteration of Greek *xērion*, a medicinal powder, from
xēros, dry. Also noteworthy is *elemi*, a resin drawn from
any one of various tropical trees. English has adopted
elemi from Spanish *elemi*, a reshaping of Ar. *al-lāmi*, the
balsam tree. Less noteworthy is such a word as *elcaja*,
the mafura, a tree with seeds of emetic properties; *elcaja*
represents Ar. *al-qayyā'*, literally 'the emetic'. And it is
just possible that *elephant* consists of Ar. *al*, the, in its
variant form *el*, and a very early Arabic or, at the least,
Semitic re-shaping of the Egyptian source of Latin
ebur and Greek -εφας, -*ephas*, in ἐλέφας, *elephas* (genitive
elephantos); with L. *ebur* and Gr. -*ephas*, compare Egyp-

tian *abu*, Coptic *ebu*, two words meaning both 'elephant' and 'ivory'. (The ill-known yet certainly intimate inter-relationships between the Semitic languages of the Near East and the Hamitic languages of North Africa no longer need to be emphasized.) It is, in short, just possible that *elephant* stands, etymologically and elliptically, for 'the ivory-yielder' – 'the ivory-yielding animal' – 'the ivory animal'.

Usually, however, *al* appears unchanged in the English adoptions or adaptations from Arabic *al*, the + a noun; many of these terms have passed through Spanish, a language with vocabulary indelibly influenced by the Moorish conquest and occupation of Spain during the Middle Ages; occasionally with a further filtering through French. These *al-* terms are so numerous that, for convenience, I have classified them, alphabetically in each group, under Astronomy, Mathematics, Chemistry, Architecture, Amenities of Civilization, Gods and Persons (especially officials), The Animal World, Plant Life, and Miscellaneous. The influence of the great medieval Arabic scientists and inventors upon the vocabulary of English appears to be very considerable.

ASTRONOMY. The astronomical terms deriving from Arabic fall into two groups: names of stars; and general. The stars include *Aladfar*, from Ar. *al-azfār*, the talons; the small *Alcor*, Ar. *al-khawwār*, the weak one; the famous *Aldebaran*, Ar. *al-dabarān*, the follower, from *dabar*, to follow – 'this star follows upon the Pleiades' (Webster); *Algebar*, the constellation Orion, from Ar. *al-jabbūr*, the giant; *Algol*, that fixed star in Medusa's head which, mostly shining very brightly, suddenly grows dim – from Ar. *al-ghūl*, the ghoul, *ghūl* (whence *ghoul*, hence *ghoulish*) deriving from *ghāla*, to seize; *Almuredin*, 'probably from Ar. *al-murīdīn*, the aspirants' (Webster); *Al*

Naṣl, the arrow-head, or the sword-blade; *Alnath*, the first star in the horns of Aries, Ar. *al-naṭḥ*, the act of goring, or of butting, with the horns; *Alnilam*, corruption of *Alnitham*, Ar. *al-naẓm*, the string of pearls; *Alnitak*, Ar. *al-niṭāq*, the belt; *Al Niyat*, Ar. *al-niyāṭ*, the aorta veins; *Altair*, Ar. *al-ṭa'ir*, the flier, (hence) the bird; *Aludra*, Ar. *al-'adhra'*, the virgin. There are many other stars with Arabic names.

ASTRONOMY: *General Terms.* Only six demand mention, these being *alichel*, at first in error for *alicbel*, Ar. *al-iqbāl*, the approach; *alictisal*, Ar. *al-ittiṣal*, the adjacency or contiguity, hence the junction (root: *wasala*, to join); *almagest*, or *Almagest*, the early 9th Century Arabic translation, *al-majusti* (the greatest), of the Greek work on Astronomy, Claudius Ptolemy's *Megalē Syntaxis tēs Astronomias*, shortened to *Megistē Syntaxis*, greatest composition, *al-majusti* (corresponding to Greek *hē megistē*) becoming *almageste* in Medieval Latin and in Old French before passing to Middle English; *almucantar*, from Fr. *almucantarat*, from Med. L. *almucantarath*, a transliteration of Ar. *al-muqanṭarāt*, the arched bridges; *almury*, Ar. *al-mur'i*, the indicator; and *almuten*, an alteration of Old Fr. *almutaz*, Ar. *al-mu'tazz*, the reckoner of himself as mighty. For a general term less easily recognizable as 'articled noun', see *azimene* or *azimuth* in the paragraph on 'disguised' terms.

MATHEMATICS. *Algebra*, whence *algebraic, algebraist, algebraize*, etc., has come, via Italian *algèbra*, from Ar. *al-jabr*, reduction of parts to a whole, the reunion of (broken) parts, hence its application both to the symbolic generalities of algebra (in contrast to the concrete particularities of arithmetic) and to bone-setting; *jabr* derives from *jabara*, to bind together. Strictly, It. *algèbra* comes from the first part of the full Arabic designation: *al-jabr w-al-muqābalah*, the reduction and the comparison ('by equations' being understood); a designation occurring first in a treatise upon algebra by the Arabic mathematician, al-Khuwārizmi ('he of Khuwārizm' – the modern Khiva) early in the 9th Century, from whose name has, through Med. L. *algorismus* and then Old Fr. *algorisme*, derived *algorism*, an old word for arithmetic and a modern one for the art of calculating with any notation. The form *algorithm* shows the influence of the Gr. *arithmos*, number – an influence exemplifying a muddle-headed erudition. An *almud*, or *almude*, is an Iberian measure of capacity: Spanish *almud*, like Portuguese *almude*, transliterates Ar. *al-mudd* (the measure), a dry measure – perhaps from root *madd*, to extend or expand. Compare that Portuguese measure of capacity which is named *alqueire*, from Ar. *al-kaylah* (or *al-kailah*), the measure – from root *kāla*, to measure (liquids, cereals, stuffs), to allot.

CHEMISTRY owes much to Medieval Arabia. The principal terms, alphabetically arranged, are these: –

albetad, galbanum: Arabic *al-birzad*; Ar. *birzad* or *barzad* has been adopted from Persian *birza* or *birzay*, *berza* or *berzay*. Already in Persian, the word meant 'galbanum'.

alchemy, whence *alchemic* (Medieval Latin *alchimicus*) and *alchemist* (Med. L. *achymista*, hence Old Fr. *alquemiste*): Old Fr. *alquemie*, *alquimie*: Med. L. *alchimia*: Ar. *alkīmiya'*, itself from Late Gr. *khēmeia* (often represented as *chēmeia*), probably for *khumeia* (*chymeia*), from *khumos* (*chymos*), juice, especially that drawn from plants, *khumos* deriving from *kheein* (*cheein*), to pour: 'chemistry was originally the art of extracting medicinal juices from plants' (Webster): compare, therefore, the word *chemistry* itself.*

* For a possible – not an entirely improbable – Proper Name origin, see *Name into Word*.

I

alchitran or *alkitran,* mineral pitch, tar, liquid resin from fir trees: Old Fr. *alquitran:* Ar. *al-qiṭrān,* the tar or pitch. *Qiṭran* has variant *qaṭran,* which clearly shows the root: *qaṭara,* to trickle, to fall drop by drop, to exude.

alcohol, whence *alcoholate – alcoholic – alcoholism – alcoholize – alcoholometer* and *alcoholysis:* 'adopted from the Latin of the alchemists, *alkol, alkohol . . .*; this word is, in its turn, borrowed from the Ar. *al-koḥl,* pulverized antimony' (Bloch & Wartburg) – a powder used for painting the eyelids. The element *koḥl* or *kuḥl* – 'pronounced *kŏŏ-h'l,* accent on first syllable, the *oo* as in *book,* the *ḥ* strongly aspirated, and the apostrophe indicating a slightly neutral vowel' (Gerald Hatchman) – has yielded the independent *kohl.* Linked with *alcohol* is *alquifou* or *alkifou* (native lead sulphide), of the same Arabic origin but via Sp. *alquifol.* Related to *kuḥl* is *kaḥala,* to paint, stain (the eyelids): but *kaḥala* (cf. Hebrew *kakhal*) probably derives from the noun.

alembic: M.E. *alambic:* Old Fr. *alambic:* Ar. *al-inbīq,* the still: *inbīq,* from Gr. *ambix,* a cup, especially the cup-like cap of a still. The archaic *limbeck* or *limbec* is a modified shortening of *alembic.*

alkahest is a back-door entry: the Med. L. *alkahest,* Paracelsus's term for his 'universal solvent', is a pseudo-Arabic formation, *al* imitating the Arabic definite article.

alkali, whence *alkalify – alkaline,* hence *alkalinity – alkaloid – alkalosis:* M.E. *alkaly* or *alcaly:* Old Fr. *alcali:* Ar. *al-qili,* the ashes of the saltwort. *Qili* is probably a 'primitive' noun – one not derived from a verbal root. If, however, the noun does derive from a verb, that verb will be *qalā,* to fry. The Arabic for 'alkali' is *milḥ-ul-qili,* salt of qili.

alkanet: alcaneta, diminutive of Sp. *alcana,* from Med. L. *alchanna* (whence the Modern Latin *Alkanna*), from Ar.

al-ḥinnā', the henna; clearly *henna* comes from *ḥinnā'*, a tropical shrub whose leaves yield a reddish-orange dye. Moreover, the Arabic word that gives us *alkanet* gives us also *orcanet*, with variants *orcanette* and *orchanet*: Fr. *orcanète* or *orcanette*, diminutive of *orcanne*, earlier *arcanne*: compare the Sp. *arcaneta*, variant of *alcaneta*.

CHEMISTRY, *continued*: *alkermes, kermes; carmine, cramoisy, crimson.*

alkermes: Fr. *alkermès*: Sp. *alkermez*: Ar. *al-qirmiz*, the kermes insect, hence (in old pharmacy) a cordial based thereon. And *kermes* itself comes, via Fr. *kermès*, from Ar. *qirmiz*; *kermes* yields *kermesite* because of the colour-resemblance; compare *crimson, cramoisy, carmine*, for Ar. *qirmiz* (itself, by the way, from Sanskrit *krmi*, an insect, a worm) leads to Sp. *cremesín*, whence *crimson* – *qirmiz* has derivative *qirmizî*, red of the kermes insect, whence It. *chermisi*, or *cremisi*, and Sp. *carmesi*, whence, perhaps by confusion of the Italian and Spanish forms, the Fr. *cramoisi*, whence the archaic English *cramoisie* or *cramoisy*; and *qirmiz*, blended with L. *minium*, yields Med. L. *carminium*, whence Fr. *carmin*, whence *carmine*. Concerning Ar. *qirmizî*, Bloch & Wartburg remark that it 'is found also in the Byzantine Greek *khermezi*; but the paths followed by the Arabic word in its diffusion have not been clearly determined'.

CHEMISTRY, *concluded*: *almagra, aludel.*

almagra, a purplish-red ochre found in Spain: Sp. *almagra*: Ar. *al-maghrah*, the red earth, from *maghra*, russet colour.

aludel, a pear- or bottle-shaped pot: adopted from French, which adopted it from Spanish, which transliterated Ar. *al-uthāl*, the utensils or apparatuses, *uthāl* being apparently a variant of *ithāl*, plural of *athlah*, utensil.

amalgam, a metal alloy, comes from the Fr. *amalgame*,

from Medieval Latin *amalgama*, a re-shaping of Ar. *al-malgham*, the kneading or softening; the second element, however, has been borrowed from Greek *malagma*, from *malassein*, to soften, itself from *malakos*, soft. The chief subsidiaries are 'to *amalgamate*' and *amalgamation*.

anatron, obsolete for 'natron', has been adapted from Sp. *anatrón*, itself from Ar. *al-natrun*, 'the natron' – native sodium carbonate. The Arabic word is akin to *nitre*.

antimony (adjectives *antimonic, antimonious*) certainly comes from Med. L. *antimonium*, which apparently comes from Ar. *al-uthmud*, variant *al-ithmid*, 'the antimony'. The alteration from *al-uthmud* (*-ithmid*) to *antimonium* is formidable: but those medieval alchemists did, with words, things almost as strange as they did with metals and minerals.

ARCHITECTURE. There are only four terms of note.

First, *alcántara*, a bridge: a barely acclimatized word adopted from Spanish, which merely transliterated Ar. *al-qantarah*, the bridge, from *qantara*, to knit together, hence (modern) to vault, to arch; the noun is 'probably of medieval date only', for 'the classical Arabic for "bridge" is *jisr*' (Gerald Hatchman). The Spanish city of *Alcántara*, situated near the Portuguese frontier, refers, by its name, to that magnificent bridge which was built, by the Emperor Trajan, over the Tagus; and Portuguese *Alcántara*, now part of Lisbon, refers to a very fine aqueduct.

The *Alcazar* of Seville is a particularization of Sp. *alcazar*, a fortified place, hence, in the Middle Ages (and predominantly later), a palace: Ar. *al-qasr*, the fortress, the castle: most of the early castles were strongly fortified. The noun *qasr* (not *qasr*, force, compulsion) exhibits the fame of Rome: it alters L. *castrum*, a fortified place. For the stem, compare *alcazava*.

Like *alcántara* barely acclimatized, *alcazava* (or *-aba*), a fortress, is Sp. *alcazaba*: Ar. *al-qaṣabah*, the fortress. *Qaṣabah*, a fortress, perhaps derives from *qaṣaba*, to cut off:? 'place cut-off from its surroundings'. Clearly related is *Kasbah* or *Casbah*, especially that at Algiers and that at Tangiers; in North Africa, *Kasbah* designates the high, fortified parts of a city, the sense 'disreputable quarter' being a British and American soldiers' debasement: *Kasbah* represents Ar. *Qaṣbah*, particularization of *qaṣbah*, a citadel.

Alhambra, whence *Alhambresque*, is the Spanish name of the Moorish kings' alcazar at Granada: Ar. *alḥamrā'*, the red ('edifice' or 'house' understood), a name deriving from the colour of the walls of the citadel-palace: walls built, in the main, of beaten earth.

AMENITIES OF CIVILIZATION. The chief, perhaps, of these derivatives from Arabic are: —

alboronoz, a Moorish cloak, clearly represents Ar. *al*, the + Ar. *burnus*, a burnous.

albricias, a reward to a bringer of good news, is used in Spanish America: Sp. *albricias*: Ar. *al-bishārah*, the good news, hence a gift to the bringer, hence a gratuity bestowed in such circumstances. The root is *bashira*, to rejoice at, be delighted with.

alcarraza, a porous-earthenware vessel: Sp. *alcarraza*: Ar. *al-karrāz* (or *kurāz*), or, in some local pronunciation, *ıl-karrāz*, the bottle or flask. 'Probably *kur(r)āz* is an Arabic borrowing of Persian *karrāz*, jug, narrow-necked goglet, earthen vessel without handle, small bottle or phial. The forms *kurāz*, *kurrāz* are not those of normal Arabic nouns' (Hatchman).

Alcoran, the Koran: via Spanish from Ar. *al-qur'ān*, the recitation (or reading).

alcove: Fr. *alcôve*: Spanish (and Portuguese) *alcoba*: Ar. *al-qubbah*, the dome or cupola or arch or vault, hence –

in the Western European languages – an 'arched' or canopied room. 'In the Mesopotamian dialect, *qubbah* means "room". Root, *qabba*, to jut out, to swell or bulge' (Hatchman). Compare the Persian *qubbah*, dome, vault, arch.

alfin, obsolete for the Bishop in chess: Old Fr. *alfin*: Sp. *alfil*: Ar. *al-fīl*, the elephant (original form of the piece).

aliofar, obsolete for a seed pearl: Sp. *aljófar*: Ar. *al-jawhar*, the matter, substance, element, (hence ?) gem, jewel.

aljama, a Jewish congregation in medieval Spain: Ar. *al-jamāʿah*, the assembly (of people). Root: *jamāʿa*, to gather, collect, bring together. Not to be confused with: –

aljamía,* the vernacular Spanish that is spoken by either Jews or Moors: Ar. *al-ʿajamīyah*, that which is non-Arabic, hence foreign. The simple noun for 'foreigner' is *aʿjami*; *ʿajamīyah*, better *ʿajamīah*, is an adjective, meaning 'foreign (esp. Persian), non-Arabic'. The root is *ʿajama*, to bite, to gnaw, whence *aʿjama*, to speak barbarously, unintelligibly. 'Incidentally, Arabic has also a verbal root *barbara*, to talk indistinctly, jabber, whence *Barbar*, a Berber; *Barbaría*, Barbary' (Gerald Hatchman) – probably the verbal root is a borrowing from Gr. *barbarizein*, to speak gibberish (cf. *barbarian*).

almadia or *almadie*: Port. *almadia* and, from *Portuguese*, the Fr. *almadie*: Ar. *al-maʿdīyah* or *-maddīyah*, the ferry-boat: *al*, the + *maʿdīyah* or *-maʿddīyah*, a ferryboat – perhaps from *ʿadd*, to count, but probably from *ʿaday*, to cross, or *ʿadday*, to cause to cross (Hatchman). Among sailors, either *almadia* or the less general *almadie* denotes,

* This *al*- is strictly not the Arabic article but the Spaniards' modification of the (to them) unpronounceable letter *ain*, loosely called 'a single inverted comma'.

in Africa, a bark canoe and, in India, a narrow boat
some eighty feet long. In Spanish, *almadía* has also the
meaning 'raft'.

almanac, almanach: M.E. *almenak*: Med. L. *almanac(h)*:
Spanish Arabic *al-manākh*, almanach, calendar: native
Ar. *al*, the + *manākh*, weather, climate, *manākh* consisting of *ma-*, a prefix connoting a place, and *nākha*, to
kneel down: a place where camels (habitually) kneel
becomes a camp, then perhaps a regular camp, a
settlement; a settlement is a place whence weather con-
ditions can be dependably observed – weather in
general, i.e. climate.

almemar, that platform in a synagogue which bears
the reading-desk: Ar. *al-minbar*, the pulpit.

GODS; PERSONS–ESPECIALLY OFFICIALS AND
OFFICERS. *Allah* is Ar. *Allāh*, a conflation of *al-ilāh*,
the god, i.e. *the* god: God. (In modern Arabic, *al-ilāh* is
still 'the god'; *al-Ilah* still an occasional spelling of
Allah, God.) Compare the Syro-Arabian mother-
goddess *Allat*, Ar. *Allāt*, conflation of *al-ilāhah*, the goddess, perhaps ultimately akin to Assyrio-Babylonian
goddess of the underworld *Allatu*. Semitic religion
accounts also for *Aladinist*, a Mohammedan free-
thinker, from *Aladin*, European for Ar. *'Ala'-al-Din*,
literally 'the height of religion' – the name of an erudite
divine under Mohammed II. Compare the *Almoravides*,
members of an African tribe formed into a Mohammedan sect: the singular *Almoravid(e)* comes from Ar.
al-murābit, the ascetic – the person dwelling in a *ribāṭ* or
fortified convent, *ribāṭ* deriving from *rabaṭa*, to tie or
bind. Compare *marabout*: Fr. *marabou*, *marabout*: Portuguese *marabuto*: Ar. *murābit*. (From *marabout*, a Mohammedan ascetic or saint, comes the *marabou*, a large stork,
hence – from the bird's softer feathers – a kind of raw
silk. The Arabic plural *Murābitīn*, a Moorish dynasty,

yields *marabotin*, (hence ?) *maravedi*, a Spanish name for the dinar used by the Moors in Spain and Morocco.) A teacher of Mohammedan law is called *alfaqui* (or *-quin*): Sp. *alfaquí*: Ar. *al-faqīh*, literally 'the understander', from *faqiha*, to be wise. An *alcaide* is a commander of a fortress or a castle: Ar. *al-qū'īd*, the leader, from *qāda*, to lead. But an *alcalde* is a mayor (usually) or a judge: Ar. *al-qāḍī*, the judge, from *qaḍa*, to decide. Compare *cadi*, an inferior judge or magistrate among the Mohammedans. An *alquazil* (or *-cil*) was so named in medieval and (*-cil*) in modern Spanish: from Ar. *al-wazīr*, the vizier (cf., therefore, *vizier*). In the Spanish army, an ensign used to be *alferes* or *alferez*: Ar. *al-fāris*, a cavalier. One of the titles assumed by Mohammedan rulers was *Al-Mansur*, less strictly *Al-Mansour*: *al-mansūr*, literally 'the aided one', hence 'the man given victory, the victorious' (cf. *naṣr*, victory, from *naṣara*, to aid, help). Hence, in Dryden's *The Conquest of Granada*, the egocentric knight-errant, *Almanzor*. In the *Arabian Nights*, the barber's foolish-investor, infatuated-dreamer brother was named *Alnaschar*: Ar. *al-nashshār*, the babbler, *nashshār* meaning literally 'sawyer', hence (*quelle scie!*) 'babbler'; *nashār* derives from *nashar*, to spread, scatter, saw.

ANIMAL LIFE. Mohammed, in journeying at midnight to the seven heavens, rode on *Alborak*, a winged, milk-white creature with peacock's tail and woman's head: Ar. *al-burāq*, the shining, the flashing, hence the shiner, from *baraqa*, to glisten, flash, shine brilliantly. Back to earth, we note that *algazel*, an antelope – especially a gazelle – of Africa, was originally Ar. *al-ghazāl*, the gazelle: *gazelle*, indeed, comes from Ar. *ghazāl*. One of the handsomest gazelles is the Persian, well known in Arabia too. There remain a fish, *albacore*, and two birds, *albatross* and *alcatras*. The *albacore*, a large fish, e.g. the tunny, has, via Port. *albacor*, taken its name, perhaps, from the Ar. *al-bakr* (or *-bukr*), literally 'the (*al*) young camel', for some rather fancifully superficial reason – probably the large size of the fish, as Ernest Weekley has suggested. But 'the albacore was certainly not called *al-bakr* (the young camel) in Arabic – in fact, I am not sure why O.E.D. derives *albacore* from *al-bakr*, unless that is supposed as the root of the real Arabic word for the fish, which is *bakura*' (Hatchman). *Alcatras*, originally the pelican ('whose beak holds more than its belly can'), then any of several large water birds, now predominantly the frigate bird: Port. *alcatraz*, originally the pelican, then cormorant or albatross (compare Sp. *alcatraz*, pelican): Port. *alcatruz*, a bucket: Ar. *al-qādūs*, the jar, the bucket of a water-wheel: Gr. *kados*, a water vessel, a water jar: perhaps of Semitic origin (cf. Hebrew *kad*, water jar): 'basic idea: water carrier' (Webster). The O.E.D. aptly recalls that a modern Arabic name is *saggā*, a normal dialect variant of *saqqa*, 'water-carrier'. And *albatross* is a corruption, influenced by L. *albus*, white, of *alcatras*; the adult bird is white. Note that Ar. *qādūs* has a transferred sense – that of 'albatross'.

PLANT LIFE. Several aromatic plants are called *albahaca*, adopted from Spanish, which thus, by metathesis and by the addition of a final *a*, distorted the Arabic *al ḥabaq*, the pennyroyal, basil; Spanish has the variant *alhábega*. The fragrant resin known as frankincense has another name, *olibanum*, adopted from Medieval Latin, which thus transliterates the Ar. *al-luban*. With *luban*, compare the Greek *libanos*, incense-tree – a word clearly of Semitic etymology. The shortened form *oliban* is simply an adoption of the French shape of Med. L. *olibanum*. *Albardine*, esparto, has, through Sp. *albardín*, come from Ar. *al-bardī*; *al*, the + *bardi* or *burdi*, esparto, probably from Persian *bardi*, reed papyrus.

Alcornoque, the bark of several trees, including the cork tree, derives from Sp. *alcornoque*, the cork tree: but we lack any evidence that the Spaniards drew it from an Arabic word beginning with *al*, the. (They probably didn't.) The forage plant lucerne is also – and in the U.S.A. mostly – called *alfalfa*, which is a Spanish word, an adaptation of Ar. *al-fişfişah*, the lucerne; Gerald Hatchman thinks that *fişfişah* may be an imitative reduplication. *Alfilaria* or pin grass or, botanically, erodium, is a Mexican Spanish word, derivative from European Sp. *alfiler*, a pin, itself from Ar. *al-khilāl*, the thorn, the prickle, hence the wooden pin or peg, the skewer, from *khalla*, to pierce, hence to pin. And Sp. *alfiler* has a diminutive *alfilerillo*, used as a synonym both of *alfilaria* and for Mexican (or hedge-) cactus.

PLANT LIFE, *continued*: *Algarroba* is a Spanish name for the carob, the honey mesquite, the rain tree, etc.: Ar. *al-khurrūbah*, the carob; *kharrūbah*, via Fr. *caroube*, yields *carob* itself; and Fr. *caroubier*, carob tree, has passed into English with the sense 'colour of Russian calf'. Now, Sp. *algarroba* has diminutive *algarrobilla*, adopted into English as a collective term for such seeds and pods of leguminous trees as are used in tanning and dyeing; *algarroba* also yields the dye-stuff *algarrobin*. *Alhagi* is the Scientific Latin name for a small genus of desert shrubs, including the camel's-thorn (*Alhagi Maurorum*, literally 'of the Moors'): Ar. *al-hāj*, the camel's thorn. *Alkekenji* is the Medieval Latin name for the ground cherry or its fruit: Ar. *al-kākanj*: Ar. *al*, the + Persian *kākanj*, a resin from Herat. A certain tall Philippine tree that produces a valuable resin (hence, the resin itself) is called *almáciga*, Spanish for the mastic tree: *almáciga* consists of Ar. *al*, the + *maştakā* (or *muştakay*) – an Arabic re-shaping of Gr. *mastikhē* (whence *mastic*). *Almáciga* is 'a simpler and more popular form of *almástiga*. The Arabic *al-maştakā* (mastic), where the *al* is the Arabic definite article, has been borrowed from Greek, or from later European derivatives. Apparently Spanish got its present word by a roundabout route through Arabic, hence the *al-'* (Hatchman). 'The connection of the Greek word with the idea of "chewing" [*massein*, to chew; *mastikhē*, chewing gum] is exactly parallelled by the native Arabic *'ilk*, mastic, gum, resin, from the root *'alaka*, to chew' (Hatchman). The madder of the Levant is technically known as *alizari*, adopted from French, which took it from Spanish, which apparently transliterated Ar. *al-aṣārah*, the juice, itself from *'aṣara*, to squeeze, press (out). And the Fr. *alizari* has the derivative noun *alizarine*, presumably the feminine of an adjective *alizarin*: in British chemistry, the form of the noun – adopted from French – is either *alizarin* or, less usually, *alizarine*.

A 'disguise' at first conceals the Arabic connexion of *anil* – whence *anilic, anilide, aniline*. *Anil* has passed through French and, earlier, Portuguese *anil*, from Ar. *al-nīl*, 'the indigo plant', hence 'indigo'. Arabic took the word from Sanskrit: *nīlī*, indigo, itself a derivative from *nīla*, dark blue – a word that happens to constitute the origin of *lilac*.

MISCELLANEOUS. Two Proper Names deserve to be mentioned: *Guadalquivir* and *Gibraltar*. The former is an Hispaniolized re-shaping of Arabic *al-wad il-kabīr*, literally 'the river the big' – the big river, the biggest in Spain; the article *al* has been dropped, and *kabīr* is pronounced almost exactly *kebir* (cf. Arabic *jabal*, pronounced *jebel*). The latter is *al-jabal Uṭ-Ṭāriq*, the mountain of At-Ṭāriq. The change from *al* to *il* in *il-kabīr*, like that of *Aṭ* to *Uṭ-Ṭāriq*, follows general rules of Arabic morphology – cf. Italian *dello* for *de il(lo)* or French *des* for *de les*. Compare, further, the *Kasr el-Nil* Barracks on the Nile: strictly, *Qaṣr ul-Nīl*. – Very different from *Gibraltar* and *Guadalquivir*, but, in some respects, comparable to what has happened in *Allah*, is the case of *hoi polloi* (Greek οἱ πολλοί), 'the many' (men, hence persons) – the multitude. The odd thing is that *hoi polloi*, when used in English, is, except by Grecians, apprehended as an indivisible noun; that is, as if it were written *hoipolloi*; and it occurs in such contexts as 'What does culture matter to the *hoi polloi?*' CONCLUSION. Within Arabic, there is only one instance (*Allah*: page 121) of the fusion of the article *al* with the ensuing noun. But certain European languages – most notably (and probably the earliest) Spanish – have incorporated *al* with a noun. 'In Arabic, the article is usually prefixed, as in French, to abstract nouns used in a general sense, e.g. "*The* bravery is a virtue". This accounts for *al-ittiṣāl* [see *alictisal* above]. The same applies to the names of materials, flowers, and other nouns used in a general sense, e.g. "*The* man is mortal" and "*The* gold is yellow". Hence *al-ḥabaq* (cf. *albahaca*), *al-bardi* (*alabardine*), *al-qādūs* (for *albatross*), *al-birzad* (*albetad*), *al-kuḥl* (for *alcohol*), *al-qaṭrān* (*alchitran*) and several more. Naturally the article is prefixed, to denote, as in English, the specific as distinguished from the general, hence *al-qanṭarah* (cf. *alcantara*), *al-qaṣr* (*alcazar*), *al-qasabah* (*alcazava*), etc., referring to specific castles and bridges. This usage includes examples, also parallel with English, where a participle is applied adjectivally to a particular person, hence *al-burāq* (*Alborak*), *an* (= *al*)-*nashshār* (*Alnaschar*) and *Al-manṣūr*. In all these words it is easy to account for the use of *al* in Arabic itself, and I suggest that, as the Spaniards in particular would seldom hear the words apart from the Arabic article, they would be led to adopt the article-noun combination *in toto* because they "felt" it to be inseparable. Your list, however, includes six words in which the article would not be inevitably attached in Arabic; these are *kurāz* (*alcarraza*), *qubba* (*alcove*), *maʿadīyah* (*almadia*), *mudd* (*almud*), *kailah* (*alqueire*), and *athlah* (*aludel*). Here I can only suggest that they and their like were treated in the same way by the Spaniards by analogy with the others, because, although they would not always hear the Moors use the article in these words, they would sometimes hear it. . . . I should be inclined to think that the practice started with the Spaniards, that it was reproduced automatically in English and other borrowings-through-Spanish of the Arabic words, and that all the European languages borrowing direct from Arabic incorporated the article *al* because it formed a necessary part of the expression – or they thought it did.' (Gerald Hatchman.)

POSTSCRIPT. Two unusual formations are exemplified in *admiral* and *botargo*. The latter, denoting a relish of mullet – or tunny – roes, has been adopted from Italian, which adapted Arabic *biṭrākhūn*, the plural of *baṭrakhah*, an adaptation of Coptic *outarakhon*, itself a merging of the Coptic indefinite article *ou*, a, an, and Greek *tarikhion*, pickle, as Webster has made clear. Now, *tarikhion* (τάρίχιον) is the diminutive of *tarīkhos*, anything artificially pickled: cf. *tarīkheuein*, to preserve, embalm, pickle, akin to *tarkhuein*, to bury in the earth. In its different way, *admiral* is equally remarkable. The Middle English forms *admiral, amiral*, were adopted from Old French *admiral, amiral*; the former shows the influence of Latin *admirabilis*, admirable; the latter, or 'true', form transliterates Arabic *amīr-al* (commander of the) – a stopping-short of Ar. *amīr-al-baḥr*, commander of the sea. This *amīr-al-* occurs in other Arabic titles. In French, the earliest form was *amiralt*, whence *amiralte*, later *amiralté*, whence – but influenced by *admiral* – the English *admiralty*. (In the 17th Century, the adjective *admirable* became, for a generation, *admiral*.) The Ar. *amīr*, meaning also a chief, was adopted into English, with variant *ameer*, but is now obsolete, being superseded by *emir*, rare variant *emeer*; hence *emirate* – an emir's state or jurisdiction. For the entire *admiral-admiralty* group and the *admiral-admirable* confusion, the O.E.D. entries are thoroughly illuminating.

(This article was written in mid-1950 and enlarged, to a truer representativeness, in July, 1951.)

WESTWARD TO THE FORTUNATE
ISLES

Maybe paradise will just keep slippin' west down the
Ohio. There's an old story about heaven lyin' westward
that the poets have always told. – Hervey Allen, *Toward
the Morning*, 1948. (A tale of Pennsylvania in the 1760's.)

THE general notion of happiness after death is, in
many religions, whether Western or Eastern, linked
with – and often confused by – the notion of a heaven
upon earth. Man's reason would appear to whisper to
him, Nothing can be worse, something must be much
better, than the region where we live; especially, than
the life that is our lot. There must, therefore, exist somewhere a pleasanter region and an easier life. As in
heaven, paradise, elysium, so in those earthly utopias,
the body feels no pain, but only well-being; the mind
has peace; the spirit is serene.

Omitting, therefore, the heavens beyond the earth,
the heavens of religion, we notice that most of the
earthly Edens, belonging to literature rather than to,
although not excluding, religion, are reserved – initi-
ally, at least – for those who have lived both courage-
ously and decently; this feature characterizes not only
the Fortunate Isles but also the Celtic Avalon, to
select but one of many. If, to us, a perhaps excessive
attention seems to be paid to heroes, and if the virtual
exclusion of women raises several problems, we must
remember that these heavens on earth were not con-
spicuously logical and that they were not woman-made.

The chronological treatment of the legend of *Hai
Makarön Nēsoi*, the Isles of the Blest, named by the

Romans *Fortunatorum* – but usually *Fortunatae* – *Insulae*, the Isles of the Fortunate, the Fortunate Isles, will show that the development of the legend falls into several well-marked stages. At first, it was poetical and, in small part, religious; then historical and philosophical, only reminiscently religious; finally, historical and geographical. Late into the second, or early into the third period, came the Latin importations from Greek.

It is, however, worth noting that, from the viewpoint of religion, the moon 'was the first dwelling of the Blessed, and there lay the Elysian Fields of the poets, Proserpina's kingdom where rest the shades' or disembodied spirits of the dead. 'And the Fortunate Islands, of which the ancients sung, were no other than the sun and the moon, celestial lands bathed by the waters of the ether' (Franz Cumont, *After Life in Roman Paganism*, 1922).

The Classical Tradition*

The first or mainly poetical period opens, probably in the 9th Century B.C., with Homer, who in *The Odyssey* (IV, 561–9) originates, casually yet germinally, the later Greek belief in a group of Islands of the Blest. The 'old man of the sea', speaking in the idiom of William Morris, says to Menelaus, son-in-law of Zeus:

> To thee it shall not come
> In the horse-kind land of Argos to meet thy death and doom;
> But unto the fields Elysian and the wide world's utmost end,
> Where dwells tawny Rhadamanthus, the Deathless thee shall send,
> Wherein are the softest life-days that men may ever gain;
> No snow and no ill weather, nor any drift of rain;
> But Ocean ever wafteth the wind of the shrilly west,
> On menfolk ever breathing, to give them might and rest.

* A good list of Classical sources appears in Maurice Besnier's *Lexique de géographie ancienne*, 1914.

Concerning that passage, four points are to be noted: as every scholar knows, 'Ocean' is the Atlantic Ocean; the 'snow . . . rain' passage is translated by A. T. Murray (Loeb Classical Library) as 'No snow is there, nor heavy storm, nor ever rain'; this is a heaven on earth, not a heaven beyond the skies; 'Admission to this blissful region is not, so far as we can see, obtained by merit, but only by grace of the immortals. . . . The poet conceived of Elysium as a kind of inferior heaven. . . . There is no more religious import in the Homeric Elysium than can justly be attributed to the Epicurean heaven,' as James Adam has written in that invaluable work, *The Religious Teachers of Greece*, published in 1908 – a year after his untimely death at the age of forty-seven.

Here, we may recall the fact that Cynewulf, who was writing his poetry in ca. 870–890, imitated Homer on several occasions; most notably in *The Phoenix*, concerning the Oriental home of that fabled bird, thus:

> That is a winsome plain, the woods are green,
> far-stretching 'neath the sky. Nor there may any rain,
> nor snow, nor breath of frost nor blast of fire,
> nor storm of hail, nor fall of rime, nor torrid weather,
> nor winter shower work harm a whit; but the plain
> endureth blessed and wholesome.
> (Charles W. Kennedy, *The Poems of Cynewulf*—
> very slightly modified.)

There we have an elaboration, more poetical than logical, of the Homeric lines; an adaptation of Pagan to Christian ends. Much as Classical philosophy, by rationalizing the ancient poets, set 'the gardens fair of Hesperus' in 'the broad fields of the sky', so medieval philosophy transferred to the Garden of the Hesperides

K

and to the Isles of the Blest (the two were frequently
identified) certain characteristics of the Christian
heaven; or rather, re-invested those localities with these
properties, for St Ambrose (? 340–397) had already
described the celestial fields of bliss in terms clearly
owing much to Pindar's account of the Isles of the Blest;
other early Christian writers owed hardly less, either
to the same source or to Homer or Hesiod, as the late
Robert Eisler indicated in an erudite letter to *The Times
Literary Supplement* of September 22, 1945.

'In Hesiod [8th Century, B.C.], as little as in Homer,
are the miseries of human life alleviated by the prospect
of a happier existence after death. The earthly paradise
of which we read in the *Works and Days* – the so-called
"islands of the blest" – is . . . reserved for a few divine
favourites of the heroic age' (James Adam). To these,
'father Zeus the son of Cronos gave a living and an
abode apart from men, and made them dwell at
the ends of the earth. And they live untouched by
sorrow in the islands of the blessed [ἐν μακάρων νήσοισι,
en makarōn nēsoisi: the first time the phrase was used]
along the shore of deep-swirling Ocean, happy heroes
for whom the grain-giving earth bears honey-sweet
fruit flourishing thrice a year' (the Loeb translation by
Hugh Evelyn-White).

Thus far, then, in Greek literature, only such heroes
as, not slain in battle nor lost at sea, have been – quite
arbitrarily – favoured by the Olympian gods, go to the
Isles of the Blest. Pindar (522–448 B.C.) changes this
inequitable dispensation. In *The Olympian Odes* (II,
68–75) he tells us, via the scholarly Sir John Sandys,
that all those who 'have thrice been courageous in
keeping their souls pure from all deeds of wrong, pass
by the highway of Zeus unto the tower of Cronus, where
the ocean breezes blow around the Islands of the Blest,

and flowers of gold are blazing, some on the shore from radiant trees, while others the water fostereth; and with chaplets thereof they entwine their hands, and with crowns, according to the righteous councils of Rhadamanthys'. In Fragments Nos. 129, 130, forming a dirge, Pindar speaks of 'meadows red with roses' – of 'golden fruits' – and of the fragrance 'ever shed' over 'that lovely land': themes to which he recurs in Fragments 131 and 133. But the passage quoted in full demands a citation of two comments made, with a most pertinent erudition, by that admirable scholar, the late Dr Lewis Farnell, in *The Works of Pindar* (3 vols., 1930–32). Concerning verse 70 ('the highway of Zeus') he wrote that ' "The road of Zeus" has a mystic tone, but we cannot trace the source of the idea: it may suggest that Zeus frequently journeys to the Happy Islands to have communion with the blessed spirits'; concerning the next verse, he remarked that 'Pindar gives no indication of geography here, but the Happy Islands were probably imagined by him somewhere in the balmy West, and Kronos was prominent in the western Mediterranean'.

Early in the second stage, we find Herodotus (484–425 B.C.) saying that the Great Oasis of Khargeh – as, very much later, it came to be known – 'is called, in the Greek language, the Island of the Blest' (A. D. Godley): unimportant in itself, this reference gains an extrinsic importance from the mere fact that it is so casually indicative of a transferred sense of the phrase, the allusiveness being comparable to that of Tennyson's 'She desires no isles of the blest' and the casualness to that of Apollodorus (ca. 195–120 B.C.) when, in *The Library* (III, X, 1) he refers to 'Lycus, whom Poseidon caused to dwell in the Islands of the Blest'.

Far more important, spiritually, is the link between

Pindar and Plato. Pindar's 'conception of immortality is almost unique in literature until we come to Plato. . . . We must turn to the Platonic myths . . . in order to find a parallel to Pindar's representation of the happiness in store for virtue' (James Adam): earthly virtue rewarded after death. Yet Plato's references to the Isles of the Blest are disappointingly brief. Extremely cursory allusions occur in *The Symposium* (179 e) and in *The Republic* (VII, 519 c). The latter work, however, does (540 b of the same Book) contain the notable idea that 'when each generation has educated others like themselves to take their place as guardians of the state, they shall depart to the Islands of the Blest, and there dwell' (Paul Shorey). In *Gorgias* (523 b) we hear of the 'law' that 'the man who has lived a just and holy life shall go, when he dies, to the Islands of the Blest to dwell there in perfect happiness out of the reach of evils' (F. G. Plaistowe).

Before passing to the final stage of the Classical legend, the stage of the anecdotal historians and of certain early geographers, we should do well to interpose two mentions by Latin writers, with the caution that, the Romans having no belief in a heaven on earth, those mentions are purely literary. In *Trinummus*, at the passage that begins at verse 549, *Sicut fortunatorum memorant insulas*, Plautus (254–184 B.C.), in his robustly humorous way, causes one of the characters to remark,

'Just as they tell us of the islands of the blest where all meet together who have lived virtuously; so, on the other hand, it would be a good plan to banish evil doers to your farm, since it is such a hell on earth' (H. O. Sibley & F. Smalley).

In the *Epodes* (XVI) Horace, who lived 65–8 B.C., has written a long and beautiful description of life in

The fields of Paradise, the Islands of the Blest,
Where yearly the soil without tillage bestoweth the harvests
    unfailing,
Where blossoms aye the vine by pruner's knife un-
    dressed:

The olive shoot burgeons, the husbandman's trust it
    betrayeth never:
Dark-emerald figs begem the trees engrafted there:
Out of the holm-oak's hollow the gold of the comb drips
    ever:
With tinkling foot the rill leaps down its mountain
    stair:

a blessèd land,

For still the King of Heaven there tempers sun and rain—

as, in *The Epodes of Horace*, Arthur S. Way translates
this passage so skilfully adapted and elaborated by
Horace from Homer and Pindar.

The anecdotal historians and the early geographers
come last: they link the myth with geographical discovery. Strabo (63 B.C.–A.D. 21) speaks – Book III,
ch. ii – of the abode of the just in the Elysian Fields as
having a pleasantly temperate climate with soft, warm
winds and as being situated at 'the ends of the earth'
and of the Isles of the Blest as lying 'not far from the
extremes of Mauretania' – 'extremes' that are 'opposite
to Gades' or Cadiz. Pomponius Mela (ca. 1–70 A.D.)
affords a rather odd parallel, for he says that, facing
Mount Atlas, stand 'the Fortunate Isles, where the
earth produces, untended, an abundance of fruits that,
ever renewed, arrive season after season, with the result
that the inhabitants gently and calmly pass their days
more happily than do those who live in splendid cities'.
Making no reference to the myth and drawing upon

the geographical writings of Juba II, that king of Mauretania who lived ca. 50 B.C.–A.D. 23, Pliny the Elder (A.D. 23–69), in Book VI of *The Natural History*, defines the approximate position and describes the physical features of the Canaries, with which he identifies the Fortunate Isles. Associated with the Canaries are the Madeiras. The more southerly group, that of the Canaries, 'consists of seven large and six small islands. The group now known as the Madeiras . . . consists of two large and several small islands. . . . The Madeira group, 240 miles north of Teneriffe, seems also to have been known to the Carthaginians,' as William Woodburn Hyde remarks in his delightful *Ancient Greek Mariners* (New York, 1947). These two groups of islands are often confused or, at the least, treated as sub-divisions of a large archipelago having two easily discernible 'halves'. Clearly, the days of the myth are over. Perhaps the mythical element began to be recognized for myth as early as the 5th Century B.C., when Hanno the Carthaginian may, in the course of his famous voyage along north-west Africa, have touched at the Canaries; certainly during the 4th Century when the Phoenicians appear to have visited them. And even if the myth lost none of its magic, it yet lost some of its mystery; the idea of *Isles of the Blest* acquired something of reality from the Phoenician discoveries, in the sense that a probable localization resulted therefrom. It must, however, be noticed that 'neither Greeks nor Romans had sufficient faith in this land of bliss to make search for it after the fall of Carthage [146 B.C.]; and thus the effective discovery of the Canaries was left over to a king of Morocco named Juba . . . , who . . . fitted out an expedition which brought back detailed and accurate information' (Cary & Warmington).

Plutarch (A.D. 46–120) has told how, near the mouth of the Baetis in Spain – i.e. the Guadalquivir – Sertorius, exiled Roman and institutor of the independent state of Lusitania, 'found some mariners lately arrived from the Atlantic Islands. . . . They are called the *Fortunate Islands*. Rain seldom falls there, and when it does, it falls moderately; but they generally have soft breezes, which scatter such rich dews, that the soil is not only good for sowing and planting, but spontaneously produces the most excellent fruits, and those in such abundance, that the inhabitants have nothing more to do than to indulge themselves in the enjoyment of ease. The air is always pleasant and salubrious. . . . So that it is generally believed, even among the Barbarians, that these are the Elysian Fields, and the Seats of the Blessed, which Homer has described in all the charms of verse.

'Sertorius hearing these wonders, conceived a strong desire to fix himself in those islands, where he might live in perfect tranquillity, at a distance from the evils of tyranny and war.'

We cannot press very closely the matter of the wrong position given by Plutarch, – 'four hundred leagues from the African coast' – nor yet the wrong number (two) of islands. In his important work, *History of Ancient Geography*, Professor J. Oliver Thomson comments: 'Thus the old bright sunset Isles of the Blest were being lent a local habitation, though for most still an airy nothing, a place where all go who have lived pure lives'. It was on this occasion, ca. 80 B.C., that the name *Fortunatae Insulae* was first bestowed. Ptolemy, who flourished in the 2nd Century A.D., 'maps six' islands in the Canaries 'and puts them too far out' (J. Oliver Thomson); like Plutarch, he identifies (Book IV, ch. vi) the Isles of the Blest with this group. And Solinus

(3rd Century), in his geographical text-book, *Collectanea Rerum Mirabilium*, affords very little more than a plagiarism of Mela and Pliny; by his time 'the Fortunate Isles have become remote again' (J. Oliver Thomson); the Middle Ages lost all knowledge of the Canaries, re-discovered only ca. 1300 A.D.

We see, then, that the Greek conception of the Isles of the Blest was, from the 1st Century B.C. onwards until the 3rd Century A.D., fast becoming localized in the Canaries, especially in the Madeira group: but already in Herodotus we have seen that *Isle*, or *Isles, of the Blest* was a fanciful name for what we should colloquially term 'a very pleasant spot'. Of 'the great Messenian plain', J. G. Frazer, in *Pausanias and Other Greek Sketches*, 1900, has said that it is 'the warmest part of Greece, and on account of its wonderful fertility was known to the ancients as Makaria or the Happy Land'; *Makaria*, if taken along with the same scholar's reference to the modern city of Sparta, 'The gardens abound with orange-trees, which, when laden with fruit, remind one of the gardens of the Hesperides', throws us forward to those etymological considerations which must follow. Yet the Blessed Isle may not be in the West, nor the Blessed Land in Greece: it may be in the East. Thus, 'in the Babylonian story of Gilgamesh (of Elam?), the farthest places reached, "Isle of the Blest" and "Waters of Death", would seem to be Socotra ("Dvipa Sukhadhara" – island abode of bliss) and the Straits of Bab-el-Mandeb'; and 'from Alexander's time [356–323 B.C.] onwards a story grew up that there was in the "Erythraean Sea" [strictly the Red, but in practice also the Arabian, Sea] an island of the blest which seems to have arisen out of Arabian reports about Dvipa Sukhadhara (island of bliss, the modern Socotra) and native Egyptian tradition about Pa-anch. Here was placed a real Utopia' – to quote from Dr M. Cary and Professor E. H. Warmington's very readable and instructive book, *The Ancient Explorers*, 1929.

ETYMOLOGICAL EXCURSUS

Does the etymology of the Greek μάκαρ (*makar*) and ἕσπερος (*hesperos*) and of the Latin *fortunatus* contribute to the source or the nature of the Classical legend?

The least fruitful is *fortunatus*; *Fortunatae Insulae*, the Fortunate Isles, or *Fortunatorum Insulae*, the Isles of the Fortunate, the latter in imitation of αἱ μακάρων νῆσοι, *hai makarōn nēsoi*, the Isles of the Blest. *Fortunatus*, deriving from *fortuna*, (good) fortune, tends to mean 'favoured by the gods'; *fortuna*, originally elliptical for *fortuna dea*, derives from *fors*, genitive *fortis*, chance. Although the best authorities risk no etymology, yet it seems reasonable to align oneself with that French scholar (R. Grandsaignes d'Hauterive) who relates *fortuna* to *ferre*, to carry, to bear, on the ground that the goddess of fortune brings the good and the bad, the benefits and the ills. The inhabitants of the *Fortunatae Insulae* are themselves the *fortunati*.

The Greek μάκαρ, *makar*, fortunate, blest, although it does occasionally mean 'happy', is usually distinguished from εὐδαίμων, *eudaimōn*, happy. Its plural is *makares*: whereas *hoi makares* denotes the gods, superior to human griefs and cares, *hoi makares thnētoi* denotes those who have lived the good life and, now dead and therefore delivered from earth's griefs and cares, dwell in *hai makarōn nēsoi*, the Isles of the Blest. Incidentally, the derivative *makarios* signifies either 'happy' or (of the dead) 'fortunate'.

The etymology of *makar* is doubtful; originally, the word perhaps signified 'big' or 'tall' or 'powerful'.

There is something to be said for relating *makar* to
megas, great: the Indo-European root for the idea of
'large; greatness' was either *meg-*, as in Greek, or *mag-*,
as in Latin (*magnus*, etc.); the predominant Celtic shape
appears to be either *mag-* or *mac-*; compare the Sanskrit
majman, greatness, *maj-* being the stem, *-man* an abstract
suffix. In death, the good heroic man gains doubly in
stature: by dying and going to the Blessèd Isles, he
becomes as a demi-god: by becoming great, he achieves
happiness, and in happiness he achieves greatness.

In *the Hesperides*, which – their location being trans-
ported to the Far West – came to be synonymous with
the Isles of the Blessèd, we have, in the very etymology,
a link with the West. Greek ἕσπερος, *hesperos*, means
'evening' (noun and adjective); the *hesperos astēr* or
evening star, which rises in the west, yields the sense
'the west'; the noun *hesperos*, therefore, in addition to
signifying 'evening', signifies 'west', and the adjective
hesperos, like its subsidiary *hesperios*, signifies both 'of the
evening – vesperal' and 'western, occidental'. The feminine of *hesperios* is *hesperia*. From *hesperia khōra* or *hesperia gē*, western land, comes, by ellipsis, *Hesperia*, 'a
name given by the Greek poets to Italy and by the
Roman poets to Spain and sometimes to Italy' (*Webster's Dictionary*): compare Virgil, *The Aeneid*, I, 530.
But *hesperios* possesses a secondary feminine, *hesperis*; as
a noun, *hesperis* has plural *hesperides*, which, as a Proper
Noun, *hai Hesperides*, the Hesperides, denotes those
'*daughters of Night*, who dwelt in an island, *on the western
verge of the world*, and guarded a garden with golden
apples' (Liddell & Scott, in the recension by Sir H. S.
Jones). From meaning the guardian nymphs, *Hesperides*
came to mean also the garden itself: a garden, an
island, situated in the extreme west, especially in the
Fortunate Islands, which thus – although not from the

Greeks – receive the secondary name, *the Hesperidean Isles* or merely *the Hesperides*. We see, then, that the Isles of the Blest (*hai nēsoi makarōn*), the Fortunate Islands (*Fortunatae Insulae*), and the *Hesperides* might all be named, after the last of these, the Isles of the West. Further, Greek *ḥesperos* was originally Ϝέσπερος, *wesperos*, which is equivalent to Latin *vesperalis*: the stems are *wesper-*, *vesper-*: akin to the Greek and Latin words for '(of) evening' is the Teutonic *west* – a detail important for (say) *to go west*.

MODERN DEVELOPMENTS

'Ever since ancient peoples learnt to dissociate the dead from their graves, the region of the setting sun occupied their fancy as being the natural goal of man's last journey' (Cary & Warmington). Nor is the idea confined to Greece; indeed, the Greeks may have taken it from the Egyptians, although more probably it arose spontaneously among several of the peoples living on or near the Mediterranean. In *The Mauve Decade* (1926) – 'a study of American life at the end of the 19th Century' – Thomas Beer has written:

Odd, how all dying things turn to the West, the region of questions? So mourners on the Nile consigned the mummied citizen to the mercies of the West and soldiers of the recent muddy mess in upper France 'went west' to join Hiawatha, King Arthur and the ecstatic nun Petronilla who saw God descending from the West in the shape of a fishhook to lift her virgin soul into bliss.

In *N or M?*, a 'Secret Service' story published in 1941, Agatha Christie, archaeologist as well as novelist, wrote this parallel:

'Gone West', as a euphemism for dying, or being destroyed, or passing out of existence, was particularly in vogue among the British during the First World War. It will be noted that its roots go back to ancient Egypt.

In Amen-em-apt's *Teaching How to Live*, written ca. 700 B.C., there occurs the aphorism, 'How happy is he who hath reached the West and is safe in the hands of God'; the abode of the dead lay 'on the *west* bank of the Nile'.*

With the Egyptian motif of burial in the west, compare these verses (175–177) from the *Oedipus Tyrannus*, written by Sophocles and produced ca. 428 B.C. and quoted here in Sir J. T. Sheppard's vigorous and scholarly rendering:

As a bird on the wing, to the west, to the coast of the sunset god
Look! 'tis the soul of the dead that flies to the dark, nay, soul upon soul,
Rushing, rushing, swifter and stronger in flight than the race of implacable fire.

Dr Sheppard's 'the sunset god' represents the Greek ὁ ἕσπερος θεός, *ho hesperos theos*, literally 'the evening god' – i.e., Hades or death.

Here, then, we have the germ of the metaphor by which the sun, sinking and finally setting, aglow, lovely, mysterious, in the West, is the sun dying, therefore the day ending and dying, much as man's brief day ends in death, his light extinguished.

The sun's rim dips; the stars rush out:
At one stride comes the dark,

---

* Burton Stevenson's magnificent collection of *Proverbs, Maxims and Familiar Phrases*, whence I have drawn also the quotations from Thomas Beer, Agatha Christie, and Horace Greeley.

in the words of Coleridge's famous description of the onset of a tropical night. Yet, as the sun dies in glory, so man dies, to live again in the fabled land beyond that beautiful western horizon. Contributory to the metaphor is the fact that, beyond the Pillars of Hercules (Gibraltar), the Isles of the Blest lay remote from Greece, distance lending its customary enchantment; perhaps there were rumours, started by the Phoenicians, of agreeable warmth and of fertility (for instance, in oranges – the golden Hesperidean fruit); a 'heaven on earth' became a heaven beyond death; and, fact adding its piquancy, airy myth was rendered more poetic by history.

We must now consider the modern developments of the equation 'dying sun – dying man; the west as scene of the sun's death – the west as man's abode in after-life': and we cannot consider it better than by examining the phrase *to go west*. To quote from a letter written by Professor William Beare, ' "To go west" would have only the literal meaning for a Greek or a Roman. "The Land of the West" usually meant Italy, sometimes Spain.' True; neither a Greek nor a Roman would have apprehended *to go west* as a synonym for 'to die': but the quotations from Sophocles and others do show that the idea was at least implicit in the imagery of the poets, the dramatists and the grammarians.

In English literature and speech, the image of the dying sun was well established by 1400: 'It was night, the sun goeth west'. By the 16th Century, it had, by its transference to human beings, become metaphor, as in 'Women . . . are gone west'; there, the metaphor is already a commonplace.

Towards the end of the 16th Century, there entered an element of misfortune. In *Cony-Catching*, Part II, Richard Greene writes the significant words, 'So long as the foists [thieves] put their villanie in practise, that West-ward they goe, and there solemnly make a rehearsall sermon at Tiborne': from London's prison of Newgate, the condemned criminals went, in a cart, *westward* to the great gallows known as *Tyburn Tree*, situated near the present Marble Arch. Thus, *to go westward*, hence simply *to go west*, came to mean, 'to be hanged'; that is, to die in unpleasant circumstances. The underworld used the phrase well into the 18th Century, perhaps later. Even if the phrase disappeared from everyday speech, and it is by no means certain that it did, the idea probably remained in unrecorded folklore.

The revival of *to go west* in the War of 1914–1918, in the nuance 'to die in battle', hence 'to be missing, to get lost' (applied to things as well as to persons) – this revival may have been assisted by several external factors. *Webster's Dictionary* defines *go west* as 'to be killed; to die' and explains the phrase as coming 'probably from earlier American *gone west* (into unorganized territory), hence absconded, disappeared, dead'. But the British soldiers had used the phrase for two years before the Americans entered the war and for three years before the latter went into action. Nevertheless, the westward trek of American settlers, into country infested by Indians and occasionally presenting other dangers, a trek begun in the 18th and lasting until late in the 19th Century, did, I think, among those who had come from Britain (whence, for quite two centuries, most settlers had come), help to keep alive the phrase *to go west* in its sense 'to be killed'. In the War of 1939–1945, by the way, *gone west* was, except among the older men, displaced by the much less expressive *gone for a Burton*.

Despite this modern genesis, whereby *to go west*

meant successively 'to die by hanging' – 'to die either during or as the result of perilous migration' – and 'to die in battle' (hence, 'to get lost' or 'to be ruined or destroyed'), the old idea that *to go west*, as does the sun at its setting, connoted 'to die and then, for the good and the just, to dwell in the Blessèd Isles of the West' has had one relevant, even if, at first sight, rather trivial or perhaps merely incongruous, extension or deviation, itself a still more modern development: that of monetary fortune in the West. This idea is almost entirely American, for the two non-American instances, though interesting enough, are, the one unlikely to have generated the sense, the other too late to have been an adumbration. To many of the Irish migrating to the United States in the 1840's as a result of the potato famine, *to go west* did, in happy fact, come to connote 'to acquire riches or, at the least, a competence by migrating to the great Western continent', as, obviously, it may have done to others in the 17th–18th Centuries; and in Australia, in the late 19th–early 20th Century, *to go west* from the Eastern States meant 'to go west into "the wide open spaces" of the sheep country' – sheep being the main source of Australian wealth.

To Americans, at any date since the great gold-rush of 1849 and as a result partly of the wealth acquired on the Californian goldfields, partly of the vast areas rumoured to be open to development in the Western States, the idea that *to go west* was not merely adventurous and exhilaratingly healthy but also productive of quite useful dollars occurred inevitably, grew rapidly, endured and is, indeed, not yet obsolete. In his *Hints towards Reform*, 1850, that energetic and progressive journalist, Horace Greeley, exclaimed, 'Go West, young man, and grow up with the country'. Probably inspired by Greeley, John L. B. Soule, in an editorial

written, the following year, for the *Terre Haute Express*
(Indiana), employed the equally famous exhortation,
'Go West, young man, go West'; the latter, because
less restrictive than the former (the country having
long since grown up), has met with the more lasting success in vaudeville and film. The West became
golden, both in money and in opportunity.

Although this monetary conception, exemplified in
success-stories, may fairly be characterized as mun-
dane, yet – thanks, in some small part, to such senti-
mentalities as the phrase *the Golden West* and the song
*The Little Grey Home in the West** – it is not entirely
divorced from the ancient conception of the sunset god
beckoning to man and leading him to a sunset land,
the Fortunate Islands set beyond the sunset – the
Blessed Isles lying far to the West. Death opens for
man a portal to quietude and peace, to a happier life
in the Isles of the Blest, much as, in his earthly life, the
setting sun portends a period of repose. How fortunate
is he to be able to sleep, temporarily far from the
world: and how blessèd it is for him to die, eternally
removed from care and grief! O'er the earth's rim he
dips, to pass into a sunset world below the horizon
into a West for ever golden: into the Isles of the
Blessèd.

(Written in April–May, 1950. A 'popular' reduction to two-
fifths of this length served as my Christmas card of that year.)

* With words by D. Eardley-Wilmot and music by Hermann
Lohr, it was published in 1911.